T0195804

How to Get

MONEY

for Your

CLASSROOM

& School

How to Get

MONEY

for Your

CLASSROOM

& School

Frances A. Karnes & Kristen R. Stephens

Routledge
Taylor & Francis Group

NEW YORK AND LONDON

First published 2005 by Prufrock Press Inc.

Published 2021 by Routledge
605 Third Avenue, New York, NY 10017
2 Park Square, Milton Park, Abingdon, Oxon OX14 4RN

Routledge is an imprint of the Taylor & Francis Group, an informa business

Library of Congress Cataloging-in-Publication Data

Karnes, Frances A.
  How to get money for your classroom and school : advanced philosophy for kids / Frances A. Karnes & Kristen R. Stephens.
    p. cm.
  ISBN 1-59363-158-8 (pbk.)
  1. Educational fund raising—United States. 2. Education—United States—Finance. I. Stephens, Kristen R. II. Title.
  LB2825.K33 2005
  371.2'06—dc22
                    2005023961

ISBN 13: 978-1-59363-158-1 (pbk)

Graphic design production by Marjorie Parker

Contents

List of Figures

List of Appendices

Acknowledgements

Many people have assisted in the development of this book and for that we are extremely grateful. To the teachers who have shared their creative fund-raising activities with us, a special thank you is extended. There have been many colleagues who have given insights into the grant proposal writing process and our appreciation is given to them. The staff at the Office of Advancement at The University of Southern Mississippi has shared its knowledge and expertise in fund development and our information base has grown because of this.

The support staff at The Frances A. Karnes Center for Gifted Studies and the Duke University Talent Identification Program who assisted in manuscript preparation are to be commended, with a special thanks to Elizabeth Simmons for providing her technical insight. Our publisher, Prufrock Press, and the excellent editorial department offered great ideas and skills in finalizing this volume. We wish to give our appreciation to the tremendous teachers, administrators, and other school personnel who continue to give us encouragement and support for writing books focusing on their needs and challenges.

Our families continue to be our constant source of support and encouragement. To Ray, John, Leighanne, Mary Ryan, John Morris, Emma Leighanne Karnes and Rich and Jack Kozak, along with Dorothy and Alan Stephens, our deepest appreciation is given to all of you. The special guidance of Christopher J. Karnes and Karen and David Stephens will always be with us.

Acknowledgements

Part I

Introduction

> fund-raising—the act or process of raising funds
> by soliciting contributions or pledges . . .
>
> —Webster's Dictionary

The Need for Additional Funds

In the United States, education is primarily a state and local responsibility. Currently, of the more than $900 billion spent nationwide on education, approximately 90% comes from state, local, and private sources. Therefore, the federal contribution to education expenditures is only about 10%. Approximately 8% includes expenditures actually from the U.S. Department of Education, as the other 2% comes from other federal agencies such as the Department of Health and Human Services' Head Start program and the Department of Agriculture's School Lunch program. The Department of Education's $71.5 billion spent is just less than 3% of the federal government's $2.5 trillion budget (U.S. Department of Education, 2005, ¶1).

Figure 1 shows the percentage of revenues spent on education by sources for the 2002–2003 school year.

Funding for education has always been a challenge. Local, state, and federal funding is dwindling, and there are more initiatives at every level with inadequate dollars for support. New facilities and renovations are also needed because of population increases and updated building codes. In addition, with the increased emphasis on technology, further resources are required for equipment, software, and maintenance, along with the need for more space.

With the voucher system, public funds are spent in private and parochial schools, thus reducing the needed money base. Although more fiscal support could come from tax increases and school board referendums, the public generally remains resistant to such measures to increase resources for classrooms and schools.

It is evident that school personnel are in constant need of monies for a wide variety of instructional and supplementary materials including, but not limited to, classroom materials, computers and software, audiovisual materials, laboratory equipment, and books for libraries. *TIME* Magazine (Winter 2002) recently reported that U.S. elementary school teachers spend more than $1 billion a year of their own money on supplies for their classrooms, with the average teacher spending nearly $521 annually. This amount is 35% more than what the school provides them with to buy materials and supplies. In addition, first-year teachers spend the most ($701 a year) and are the lowest paid.

Programs in the fine and performing arts are also extremely underfunded. Funds are needed for students to participate in field experiences, attend cultural events, and for transportation. Playground equipment and ath-

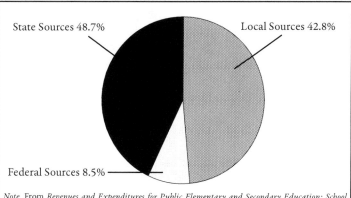

State Sources 48.7%

Local Sources 42.8%

Federal Sources 8.5%

Note. From *Revenues and Expenditures for Public Elementary and Secondary Education: School Year 2002–2003* (NCES 2005–353), by J. G. Hill and F. Johnson, 2005, Washington, DC: U.S. Department of Education, National Center for Education Statistics.

Figure 1. Revenues by source, 2002–2003 school year.

letic items must also have consideration for dollars, and new programs and initiatives continue to demand fiscal resources. Moreover, with the emphasis on performance standards, a few states and schools are hard pressed to find the necessary funds for assessment and testing of students to determine mastery of concepts and skills. These are only a few of the ongoing, and at times, overwhelming needs of schools.

There are more needs within each individual school and classroom. Scholarships are needed for both professionals and students. Teachers, administrators, media specialists, curriculum coordinators, psychologists, and counselors require grants and scholarships to attend conferences and seminars. Scholarships and stipends are also necessary for students to attend enrichment and accelerated learning experiences to enhance their education. Local and state cultural activities abound, but are usually not within the financial means of most students and schools if additional dollars are not raised. Whether urban or rural, the needs for additional funds in our nation's schools are limitless.

There are many requirements within media centers and laboratories that go beyond the set budgets of schools. Technological updates are a must, with computers and software usually at the top of the list. Print and non-print materials such as books, atlases, thesauri, videotapes or DVDs, and other instructional items need to be updated frequently, so current information is always available. Laboratory equipment and supplies are also high priorities. Consumable materials need to be replaced at a rapid pace in some areas and additional funds can always be put to good use in this way.

New buildings and additional classrooms are high-ticket items and are in constant demand as structures decay and school populations grow. Infrastructures designed in the early to the middle of the 20th century may not meet current building codes and standards. With taxpayers reluctant to pass bonds for necessary renovations and buildings, monies must be garnered through new approaches. In addition, old playgrounds may pose a danger to children. Updated equipment is necessary to maintain the health and safety of students. It is evident that construction and renovation will continue to require substantial funds, and strategic methods for securing such monies are essential.

There are usually many new programs and initiatives in need of financial resources. Character education, mediation and conflict resolution, forensic science, robotics, early reading, and parent education are but a few of the programs being added to the curriculum each year. Furthermore, there are always other projects on the horizon as determined by state and local needs.

Assessing the Need

Because of resistance from the public to increase taxes or vote for bonds, other ways of securing money must be practiced. Creative fund-raising, grant proposal writing and fund development are three ways of raising money for the school and classroom. Book fairs, bake sales, and quarter rallies are a few fund-raising ideas (Stephens and Karnes, 1999). Grant proposals can be written to public and private, local, state, and national/federal sources, while fund development involves securing private funds through annual giving, capital campaigns, endorsements, and planned giving.

To formally determine the needs of a school and/or district, a survey should be conducted. One idea would be to assess stakeholders with a survey instrument that includes all areas of potential need within the school (see Appendix A), or with one designed in a more open-ended response format (see Appendix B). The selected survey should be completed by all school personnel, current and perhaps even former students, and parents/caregivers.

With the information gleaned from the survey, a needs statement can be developed and the appropriate funding strategy formulated. Some needs may involve creative funding strategies. For example, if library books are cited as a requirement then perhaps a book fair would be a great idea to consider, with the proceeds going toward the purchase of new books. For new science equipment, a grant proposal may be appropriate to fill the need, while a capital campaign would likely be necessary if a new building or an additional wing is needed to house a fine and performing arts program.

Policies and Permissions

Whether the approach to getting money for your school and/or classroom is creative fund-raising, grant proposal writing, or fund development, there are several considerations to keep in mind. The first is to get the necessary permissions within the school and/or district. Locate a copy of the policies and procedures for raising money as approved by the school board. An important precaution is not to take the word of others without written policies, as the specifics may be lost in the translation. If written policies do not exist, request that policies be established, reviewed by the superintendent, and approved by the board. With written guidelines, there should be very specific steps and instructions regarding procedures for engaging in all areas of fund-raising.

Such policies may govern door-to-door solicitation by children for fund-raising as it becomes more hazardous than in times past. Many schools do not engage their students in this approach. If they do, specific guidelines are set forth. Even if district guidelines are established for door-to-door solicitation, it may be wise to consider other fund-raising possibilities as alternatives. Student safety should be of the utmost importance.

In the case of grant proposal writing, certain signatures for approval within the district may need to be obtained beyond those required by the agency or foundation to which it will be forwarded. In addition, the solicitation of individual donors for a capital campaign may need the approval of the superintendent and/or school board.

Another step in the process is the legality beyond school policy. If a fund-raising event is conducted off school property, are there city or county ordinances governing procedures? If raffle tickets are purchased or donations made, can these be considered as tax deductions? Are there special permits that must be obtained? These are but a few of the questions that should be considered as you begin preparing for the fund-raising process.

As with all fund-raising activities, the motivation of those involved must be reinforced and maintained. If the fund raiser is going to be a success for the school and/or district, motivation must be kept high and each victory celebrated with all who helped make it a success.

Part II

Grant Writing

An elementary school teacher secures $50,000 from a corporate foundation in her area to enhance the science lab at her school. A media specialist is awarded $200,000 from a government agency to establish a resource library for parents and teachers in his community. These are just a few examples of how grant money can help augment existing resources or establish new, innovative programs. So, what would you do for your classroom, school, or community if you had this kind of money?

Obtaining Necessary Permissions

Grants can provide schools with money for a variety of initiatives and projects, ranging in size from a few hundred dollars to millions of dollars. Educational institutions often resort to this common method of acquiring necessary funds.

Prior to beginning the grant seeking process, it is important to obtain permission to conduct the proposed project from the school administration. Be sure to allow ample time for the approval process. Start with the school principal and have he or she advise you as to other permissions that may need to be obtained at the district or board level. Once again, it is important to follow any written school and district guidelines about obtaining funding from grants.

Teamwork

Writing a grant can be an overwhelming task for anyone. However, large sums of money are often awarded, making the hard work well worthwhile. Through careful planning, the size of the task can be made more manageable. Frequently, teams are established to work together in preparing a grant proposal. Individuals who may be involved include:

- classroom teachers,
- curriculum coordinators,
- school and district administrators,
- district finance officers,
- parents,
- students,
- community organizations,
- businesses,
- university faculty, and
- concerned citizens.

While it is helpful to have a team of people working together to write grants and possibly secure funding, you may want to consider keeping the group at a manageable number. It may be difficult to develop a proposal with 20 different people working on it at the same time. You may want to survey or interview a number of people to get an idea of school or district needs or to gather information about a specific topic, but it will be helpful for you to limit the number of people who are actually in charge of preparing the grant proposal.

Funding Sources

There are multitudes of funding agencies at the local, state, and federal levels. In addition, private and corporate foundations have become a viable source of needed funds. Before preparing a grant proposal, all should be thoroughly explored to locate the best funding source for a particular project.

Public Grants

Despite the decline in funding in recent years, the federal government remains a major provider of grant dollars (Miner & Miner, 1998). Currently, the U.S. Department of Education operates programs that impact more than 14,000 school districts (U.S. Department of Education, 2005, ¶ 9). Most federal agencies have some type of grant making program.

Federal sources of funding include, but are not limited to:
- U.S. Department of Education (ED)
- The National Institutes of Health (NIH)
- The National Science Foundation (NSF)
- Administration for Children and Families (ACF)
- National Aeronautics and Space Administration (NASA)
- Environmental Protection Agency (EPA)
- National Endowment for the Humanities (NEH)
- National Endowment for the Arts (NEA)

Information regarding current federally funded grant programs can be obtained from a number of sources.

- The Catalog of Federal Domestic Assistance (CFDA)—Describes all the federal government's programs that give money. This source is published annually by the Office of Management and Budget (OMB) and is available at major libraries. [Available online at http://www.gsa.gov/fdac/queryfdac.htm]
- The Federal Register—Published every weekday except on legal holidays, it provides public regulations and legal notices issued by federal agencies. [Available online at http://www.gpoaccess.gov/fr/index.html]
- Grants.gov—An online resource that allows individuals and organizations to search and apply for more than 900 federal grants from 26 agencies. [Available online at http://www.grants.gov]

*Information on how to contact and subscribe to these publications is listed in the Resource section of this book.

Private Foundations

Private sources of funding include foundations, corporations, and professional and trade associations. There are more than 73,000 private and community foundations in the United States. By law, foundations must give away 5% of their market value assets or interest income each year, whichever is greater. If foundations do not follow this 5% rule, they can lose their tax-exempt status (Miner, Miner & Griffith, 1998). A few examples of private foundations include The Carnegie Foundation, The Kauffman Foundation, The Kellogg Foundation, and The Spencer Foundation.

Corporate Foundations

Although there are nearly 2.5 million corporations, only about one-third of them make contributions to nonprofit organizations (Miner, Miner & Griffith, 1998). Corporations tend to fund projects that will help them improve their products, lower their own costs, or improve their public image. Some examples of corporate grant makers are AT&T, Bank of America, Coca-Cola, Eastman Kodak Company, Exxon Corporation, and J.C. Penney Company.

Professional and Trade Associations

Many organizations and associations will also provide grant opportunities to individuals in their field or to those who wish to initiate projects that are of mutual interest. Examples of professional and trade associations that award grants are the American Psychological Association, The National Association of University Women, the National Council for Social Studies, The National Education Association, and Rotary International.

Check with the State Department of Education and the local school district for additional sources of funding. It is recommended that local, state, or regional sources of funding (i.e., companies and corporations with a business presence in or near the respective community and private foundations within the area) be considered first. Many such agencies require a brief letter explaining the components of the proposed project prior to submitting a formal proposal.

Information pertaining to private, community, and corporate sources of funding can be found using a variety of resources.

- *The Foundation Center* offers a collection of fund-finding publications and resources, including a database on CD/ROM with more than 50,000 foundations and more than 200,000 grants. The CD/ROM is available at the center's libraries in Washington, DC, New York, Atlanta, Cleveland, and San Francisco. To accommodate those who do not live near these locations, each state has at least one library designated to have extensive holdings from the Foundation Center. For more information, see http://fdncenter.org.
- *The Council on Foundations* is a nonprofit membership organization of grantmaking foundations and corporations. For more information, see http://www.cof.org.
- *The Chronicle of Philanthropy* is a biweekly newspaper that includes articles on fund-raising and philanthropy. Lists of recent grants and profiles of foundations and corporations are also given. For more information, see http://philanthropy.com.

*Information on how to contact and subscribe to these publications is listed in the Resource section of this book.

Selecting a Funding Agency

Careful research will ensure the selection of an appropriate funding agency for your proposed project. While the number of granting agencies may seem overwhelming, there are strategies to identify those sources that best match your need. Careful research and attention to detail can save time and help avoid potential frustrations and disappointments. Questions to consider when selecting a funding source include the following:

- *What are the priorities of this agency, and do they match the goals and objectives of the proposed project?* For example, the agency may focus their efforts in urban schools and the proposed project may be designed for a rural school system, or the agency may emphasize the incorporation of technology into the curriculum while the proposed project does not take technology into consideration. It is critical to make sure your goals and objectives match those of the funding agency. If these do not align, it is best to identify other agencies that have similar objectives.

- *What are some past projects this agency has funded?* Request an annual report from the funding agency, or visit its Web site. Most will detail current and past projects that have been funded, and patterns can be established. For example, even though the agency says they fund projects nationally, 85% of the projects funded in the past may be located in the same state or geographic region.

- *What are the limitations and restrictions?* Many agencies will not fund individuals, for-profit organizations, or political or religious groups. There may be geographic restrictions and limits to how awarded monies can be utilized. Certain types of equipment, overhead, and salaries may not be covered. Carefully read all requirements prior to drafting a proposal.

- *Is a letter of inquiry required?* Some agencies want a brief overview of the organization, goals, objectives, and expected budget of the project prior to submitting a formal proposal. A more detailed proposal will be requested if the planned idea matches the agency's priorities or agenda.

- *Are there necessary application forms or specified document formats?* Many agencies have standard application and cover forms that will need to be requested or downloaded from their Web site. Check to make sure that all proposal guidelines are addressed. Is there a page limit? Is there a requested font size or margin setting? Some agencies will discard proposals that do not adhere to their requested format.
- *What is the deadline?* Most deadlines will follow an annual pattern, but since government programs often depend on legislation for funding, many programs may be changed or dissolved. In addition, some agencies do not fund projects on an annual basis. Some foundations will often accept applications at several designated times throughout the year, while others may be willing to review applications at any time, with no established deadlines.
- *What is the average grant size?* It is important to determine the average amount of money awarded by each agency. For example, the agency may only make an award of up to $5,000, but the proposed project needs approximately $100,000 of support. Select an agency that can financially support your idea.
- *What is the length of the support?* Many federal grants will support projects for approximately 3 years, while local grants may be more short-term in nature. Continued support may be available if the project proves it has made an impact. Some funding agencies want to know how the project will be continued once funding terminates. The potential sustainability of the project is of great consideration to funding agencies as they make decisions for providing financial support.

Answers to these questions can be documented using a form similar to the one found in Appendix C (Funding Agency Prospect). If the above questions cannot be answered through a review of the agency's published materials and Web site, contact it directly for additional information. Devoting a little time to carefully researching the details of a potential funding agency is time well spent.

Letters of Inquiry

Some organizations request a letter of inquiry prior to submitting a formal proposal. The letter should be placed on appropriate letterhead and be addressed to the proper individual within the granting agency. The letter of inquiry can be the first step in getting funded by generating interest in your proposed project. Be sure to include the following information in your letter:

- A brief statement about your school, district, or organization.
- A short description of the proposed project.
- A statement regarding how the project is directly tied to the funding agency's mission.
- An explanation as to why the proposed project is needed.
- An estimation as to the amount of money needed to carry out the project. Be sure to mention in-kind contributions, too, if applicable.

Components of a Grant Proposal

The components of a grant proposal will vary according to the funding agency. Each agency usually specifies the requested components and will have maximum allowable points for each section of the proposal. The basic elements of a proposal for a foundation or corporation usually include:

- title page,
- purpose,
- plan of action,
- qualification of key personnel,
- budget, and
- attachments.

The proposals requested by state and federal agencies will require more detail and often consist of the following:

- title page,
- abstract,
- purpose,
- statement of need,
- procedures or plan of action,
- evaluation,
- dissemination,
- qualifications of key personnel,
- budget, and
- attachments.

The *title page* should include the title of the project, the legal name of the submitting agency, contact information, a brief summary of the proposed project, amount requested, signatures of approval, and other assurances such as a nondis-crimination clause. Many agencies provide preprinted forms that are to be used as cover sheets or title pages. Appendix D (Application for Federal Education Assistance) is an example of a cover sheet required by the U.S. Department of Education.

The *abstract* provides the reviewer with a succinct description of the proposed project. The goal should be to highlight those key components and areas that make the project a unique and needed endeavor. Abstracts are typically 1–2 pages; therefore, it is necessary to achieve the "best bang for the buck." This is the first component of the proposal the agency will read, so be comprehensive yet precise. If an abstract is not requested, highlight key areas of the project in the cover letter to the agency.

Questions to Answer

- Why is the project being proposed?
- Who will be served?
- What is the overall goal?
- What other organizations are involved, and what is their role?
- How does this project fit with the goals of the school, school system, and community?
- Why is your school, district, or community the best place to implement this project?
- How is the project related to the agency's funding priorities?

The *purpose* informs the granting agency what the project intends to accomplish. Focus should be on the results that will be achieved with the funding. In addition, care should be given to indicating the project's relevance to the funding source. Examples of purpose statements might include:

- Acme Unified School District plans to educate parents on the importance of providing enrichment activities at home by conducting the first community workshop on parenting for success, a topic of which your agency has an expressed interest.

- The collaborative efforts of United High School and your company have proven beneficial in reaching shared goals. Therefore, we ask that we strengthen our partnership by establishing a scholarship for outstanding minority students from our community to assist them in attending college.

The *statement of need* demonstrates to the agency the importance of the proposed project and why it is necessary. This is where the problem is explained. Statistical information derived from related research can be helpful in establishing evidence of the problem. For educators, the National Center for Educational Statistics (NCES; http://nces.ed.gov) can be a valuable resource for this type of information. Be sure to present an accurate and realistic depiction of the problem. It is important to make a clear and direct link between the problem and the goals and objectives of the project. In short, how will the proposed project specifically address the problem area?

Questions to Answer

- What is the problem?
- Why is the problem important?
- What is the need for the project?
- What does the research tell us about the problem?
- How will the proposed project address the problem?
- What makes the project innovative?
- What will make this project work?
- Who will benefit from this project?

The *procedures* or *plan of action* section details the steps that will be taken to implement and conduct the proposed project. This section presents a clear picture to the reviewer or the agency of how the project will look "in action." It is important to be as realistic as possible as to what can be accomplished. While it is easy to develop a plan of action with numerous goals and objectives that you would like to achieve with the grant money, you must keep in mind that you will be responsible for following through with all of the plans if you are granted the funding. Be sure you are not trying to accomplish the impossible.

For each objective, a time frame and the personnel responsible should be designated. It is often helpful to divide the plan of action into phases. For example:

- Phase 1—What needs to be accomplished prior to implementation?
- Phase 2—What will occur during implementation?
- Phase 3—What will happen after implementation?

For federal grants, which usually encompass 3 years, the plan of action should be organized according to each fiscal year. Never assume that the agency or reviewer completely understands the intent of your project or the tasks that are to be accomplished. Be sure to include detailed explanations of the steps you plan to take during the proposed project's timetable. The more specific you are about your plans, the better the agency or reviewer will be able to understand your project and ideas. A sample template that provides a method for presenting this information follows in Appendix E (Plan of Action). An example of a partially completed plan of action is included in Figure 2.

Goals and Objectives	Persons Responsible and Qualifications	Timeline in Months
Goal—To develop a service learning model for middle school students.		
Objective 1.0—Assemble training modules for community leaders participating in the program.	Mrs. Jones—Has had extensive experience as the coordinator of a local mentoring program.	6 Months
Objective 2.0—Develop service learning curriculum for classroom.	Mr. Smith—Has been a middle school teacher for the past 8 years, and has engaged students in service learning for the past 4 years.	8 Months
Objective 3.0—Create student handbook for service learning experiences.	Mr. Smith—See above.	2 Months

Figure 2. Plan of action completed template

Grant Writing

Questions to Answer

- What is the purpose of this project?
- What are the goals and objectives of the project?
- How will the project be implemented?
- Who will do what?
- How will each activity be accomplished?
- When will each activity be performed?
- What is the time frame of the project?

The *evaluation* section is perhaps the most important, but often neglected, component of the proposal. A sound and thorough evaluation plan can make a great proposal even stronger, but the absence of a means for evaluation can be detrimental to a proposal's acceptance. It is important to include and explain the criteria that will be used to measure success. Reviewing how similar programs have been evaluated will help you determine which criteria to use in your evaluation plan. Think through each objective presented in the procedure section and describe how each objective will be evaluated. Some objectives will involve a simple method of evaluation (i.e., feedback from a participant, completion of a phone call, or the securing of a staff member). Others may be more sophisticated and valid methods such as the administration of a standardized instrument, feedback from a consultant, or other forms of data analysis. Careful attention must be given to this section of the proposal. If the proposal has a research component involving statistical analysis, key personnel or consultants with expertise in this area need to be incorporated. Appendix F (Plan of Operation/Plan of Evaluation) demonstrates how this information might be organized, while Figure 3 provides an example of a partially completed plan.

OBJECTIVE: To disseminate information relating to the project to others across the region.

ACTIVITIES AND PERSONNEL RESPONSIBLE	TIMELINE (MONTHS)	EVALUATION CRITERIA	EVALUATION INDICATORS
Give a presentation on the outcomes of XYZ project at the ABC National Conference (Mr. Tom Smith)	March, 2006	Was the presentation accepted by ABC? Was the presentation delivered at ABC National Conference?	Acceptance of proposal by ABC and completion of presentation at the conference.

Figure 3. Plan of operation/plan of evaluation completed template

Questions to Answer

- How will each goal and objective be evaluated to assure intended outcomes?
- What will happen with the data once it is collected?
- How will data be used to improve future outcomes?
- With whom will you share your results?
- How will the results benefit others?

Dissemination of the major conclusions, findings, or results of your project is an additional area of consideration. Agencies want you to share your project with others to increase the scope of its impact. Be as specific as possible when describing selected methods for dissemination. For example, if a conference presentation will be conducted, cite the title of the session, the conference, and the date. There are numerous ways in which a project can be shared with others. A few include:

- newsletters;
- conference presentations;
- site visits;
- journal articles;
- pamphlets and brochures;
- books/manuals/handbooks;
- Web site;
- instructional modules;
- audiovisual materials (videos, television programs);
- press conferences; and
- consultation services.

Questions to Answer

- What dissemination procedures will be utilized?

- How will dissemination efforts increase the value of the project?
- For what population(s) are dissemination efforts intended?
- If materials/publications are to be produced, what is the production plan for such materials?
- How will profits from produced materials (if applicable) be handled?

Qualifications of key personnel also need to be presented. Even though résumés and professional vitae may be included in the attachments section, an explanation of how each personnel member is qualified to carry out his or her responsibilities is necessary. Elaborate on the past work and experiences of the individual that are directly related to what his or her role will be in the project. Figure 4 (Key Personnel Activities/Responsibilities) demonstrates how the responsibilities of each staff member can be displayed. See Appendix G for a blank template.

Questions to Answer

- Who will actively be involved in the project?
- What are their qualifications and expertise?
- What will each person's role and responsibility be in the project?
- How are their qualifications directly tied to their role in the project?

The *budget* is often the last item prepared in a grant proposal. Be certain that all costs are included. Worksheets are effective in organizing budget items by tying costs to

Personnel	Year 1	Year 2	Year 3
Mr. Smith	Develop a service learning curriculum for classroom.	Create student handbook for service learning experiences.	Develop evaluation instrument for assessing the impact of program on students, teachers, and the community
Mrs. Jones	Form a focus group of community leaders to generate ideas and areas of need.	Assemble training modules for community leaders participating in the program.	Conduct training sessions with community leaders.
Ms. Brown	Coordinate with teachers and schools in the community about implementation of the program.	Assemble training modules for teachers and administrators participating in the program.	Conduct training sessions with school personnel.

Figure 4. Key personnel activities/responsibilities completed template

specific activities. Some agencies, like the U.S. Department of Education, have their own worksheets (see Appendix H). In addition, it is important to take note of those items the granting agency will not cover. For example, many will not cover construction and overhead costs. Other questions to consider might be:

- Are both direct and indirect costs allowed?
- Are matching funds required?
- Once the budget is approved, are changes allowed?

Items to think about when creating a budget include:

- salaries;
- personnel benefits;
- supplies (i.e., paper, envelopes, disks, etc.);
- equipment (i.e., computers, fax, printers, etc.);
- travel/transportation;
- telephone;
- printing and copying expenses;

Terms to Know

Direct Costs—these are the line items listed in your budget as an explicit expenditure. For example, the supplies and equipment needed for a project would be included as direct costs.

Indirect or Administrative Costs—these are costs not directly listed in the budget but are incurred. These costs are usually figured as a percentage of the grant, but some foundations do not allow indirect costs to be covered. For example, the rent and utility bills for office space would be considered to be indirect costs.

Matching Funds, Cost Sharing, or In-Kind Contributions—these are the costs that your organization will contribute to the project. This may include actual cash, time, or services.

- consultant fees;
- facilities (i.e., rent, utilities, etc.);
- postage/shipping; and
- conference registration

When developing a budget, it is advisable to consult with your administration and/or finance office. A template to assist in planning a budget is provided in Appendix I (Budget Planning).

Questions to Answer

- What amount is needed to accomplish the project?
- Why is each budget item necessary to implement the project?
- Are in-kind contributions (if any) included?
- How is each budget item tied to the objectives of this project?
- How will the project be sustained after funding is terminated?

Attachments or appendices may also be included when submitting a grant proposal, although some agencies may prohibit their inclusion. Résumés, letters of support, proof of tax-exempt status, and program materials are but a few items that can be incorporated.

Handling Rejection

Try not to get discouraged if your proposal is not accepted by the selected funding agency. Grants have become very competitive, and many may not receive funding on the first try. It is advised that comments or reasons for the rejection are secured from the agency. These comments will be of great help in revising and preparing the grant for either submission to another agency or resubmission to the same one.

Celebrating Success

Writing the proposal is only part of the process. Once a proposal is accepted and funded, the work really begins. Managing a grant can be a tedious process, but the joy of your idea being liked and supported by others brings an overwhelming sense of excitement and pride. It is important to thank all the individuals who assisted in preparing the proposal and to plan a special event where you can announce the good news to all those involved.

Grant Writing: Lia Landrum's Story

Lia Landrum is a National Board Certified Teacher in Adolescence and Young Adulthood/Social Studies–History. She has received many teaching awards at the local, state, and national levels. These awards would not have been possible without grant funding to support her "out of the box" teaching style. The creative strategies utilized by this teacher demand materials other than mere pencil and paper activities and have led her to author and coauthor grants totaling more than $1 million.

She has received more than $500,000 for technology resources, including computers, multimedia equipment, and educational software. These grants have made the Jones County School District in Mississippi a technology paradise. As a result, students have become proficient in the development of multimedia presentations and research using the Internet and educational software.

Ten Tips for Writing a Winning Proposal

- Develop, document, and clearly state the specific need. Be positive and demonstrate confidence.

- Do your homework. Follow guidelines and provide all information requested by the funding agency.

- Present information in a logical, precise, and professional manner. Make appropriate use of headings and bullets to guide the reviewer to important parts of the proposal.

- Avoid jargon and explain all technical words so they are understood.

- Give specific details about what you intend to do. Never assume anything.

- Make comprehensive, realistic budgets and substantiate all figures.

- Provide evidence of your ability to undertake the project.

- Use the abstract and/or cover letter to summarize your project in a concise manner.

- Allow plenty of time to develop the proposal and obtain necessary approvals.

- Proofread and have others read the proposal before submitting it to the agency.

Other areas in which she has utilized the funding received through grants include:

- the acquisition of piano labs for three different schools, providing students who could not afford lessons the opportunity to play the piano ($30,000 from Mississippi Art Humanities Grant);
- a "Starlab" (portable planetarium) that travels around the school district teaching students about the stars, weather, and Greek mythology ($11,950 from Toshiba Foundation);
- accelerated math manipulatives, temperature sensors, and graphing calculators for geometry students ($9,000 from EDCORE, $2,000 from Mississippi Power, and several $500 awards from the Association for Excellence in Education);
- the resources needed to implement a variety of enrichment units (e.g., Architecture, Irish Culture, Leonardo da Vinci, and countless others); and
- everything from Legos to a compost bin.

Lia acknowledges that the most difficult aspect of grant writing is coming up with the two "I's," *imagination* and *innovation*. She advises that these are the elements that will distinguish your grant from all the other teachers competing for the dollars available in "Grantland." She suggests thinking of ideas that will make your grant be noticed. For example, you can integrate art, music, literature, dance, and culture with the study of history. Research on the Vietnam War can be coupled with songs of protest and propaganda. A sense of real-world connection can be attained through the development of music videos and the creation of a Beatnik Café with live performances by students.

Lia has received grants that have provided computers, research materials, café props, sound equipment, and art supplies. Parents, people representing sources of funding, students, and members of the community attended her mock café and everyone learned a great deal about the 1950s and 1960s. Granting agencies like to know that the money they provide makes a difference. Lia recommends sending pictures or a videotape of the students' accomplishments gained through awarded money to the granting agency.

Basing your grant on the *needs* of students and not the *wants* of the teacher is the best advice Lia would give a grant applicant. Ask yourself, what unit of study isn't working? What could be done to inspire students' interest in the unit? Finally, what materials are available to meet the needs? Now conclude the unit with a creative culminating activity, and you've got a grant idea!

Part III

Creative Fund-Raising

Candy, calendars, books, wrapping paper, candles, frozen entrees, greeting cards, magazine subscriptions, plants, T-shirts, coupon books, and novelty items are all familiar and popular fund-raising products. Determining what to sell can be an overwhelming process. Furthermore, fund-raising is definitely not limited to product sales. Special events can also be a great source of revenue. Whatever endeavor you decide to pursue, one thing is certain—careful planning is essential to success.

Types of Fund Raisers

There are a variety of fund-raising options:
- *Direct Sales*—asking directly for money through phone and letter solicitation, telethons, etc.
- *Indirect Sales*—selling products that have a built-in profit for the organization.
- *Events*—raising money through auctions, special dinners, "a-thons", craft shows, etc.

Status of Creative Fund-Raising in Schools

A study conducted in 2000 by the National Association of Elementary School Principals (NAESP) revealed important information on fund-raising in U.S. public schools. Seven hundred principals from urban, rural, and suburban areas in all states and Washington, DC, were represented in the study. Fifty-four percent of these principals reported conducting between one and four funding activities every year, with nearly half devoting a month or less each year on such events. In the majority of schools, the PTA/PTO is the group bearing the responsibility. Twenty-seven percent of those responding raise at least $10,000 annually. Ninety percent indicated that their schools raise money to supplement local, state, and federal funding.

How are the funds used? According to the survey, the more substantial areas of need receiving support were classroom supplies and equipment (58%) followed closely by field trips (57%). Support for library books and playground equipment was also cited. The majority of responding principals agreed the benefits of fund-raising activities far outweigh the effort and time expended, although many would discontinue the practice, if possible.

How do schools raise money? The results of the NAESP survey revealed that book fairs are employed by 88% of respondents, product sales by 81%, portraits of students/ families by 53%, and school carnivals by 48%. Some schools use year-round activities such as collection of box tops and food labels (74%), retail affiliation programs (34%), and vending machine royalties (20%).

Involving Parents

According to the principals responding to the NAESP survey, over the last 10 years there has been an increased need for fund-raising activities. With this has come a rise in parental complaints. Common criticisms include:

- the quantity and frequency of fund-raising activities,
- the opposition to having children used as salespeople, and
- concern about the quality of the products used for sales.

Parents need to be involved in the decision-making process regarding the when, where, what, and how of school fund raisers. A clear purpose for holding a fund raiser has to be communicated to parents, potential donors, and other stakeholders.

The benefits that result from past money raised should also be made evident to the public. For example, document and share how student writing achievement has increased with the purchase of new software or how the acquisition of updated laboratory equipment helped improve Advanced Placement® test scores. Once parents can weigh the potential benefits with the effort and out-of-pocket expense of holding a fund raiser, they may be more supportive of future fund-raising endeavors.

Involving Students

Bauer (2000) is a strong advocate of having students become more knowledgeable about the creative fund-raising process as a precursor to philanthropy and possible career training. Some of his ideas focus on the students' understanding of why citizens should contribute to the public schools through fund raisers when they already pay taxes. Students should be encouraged to explore what part of the cost will go directly to the school rather than the supplier, who will benefit from the monies, and what the school will provide to students with the proceeds.

Other ideas for student involvement are the selection of the goods/services to be sold and the projection of the profits. They can learn to evaluate the fund-raising activity in terms of cost-effectiveness and public relations while enhancing their math, organizational, and communication skills. Such real-world learning experiences assist students in understanding the business world and allow them to explore potential careers in marketing, advertising, accounting, writing, design, manufacturing, and more.

Sample Classroom Activities

You can bring the fund-raising process directly to your classroom by having the students participate in different projects. Students can participate in the following ways, which will benefit the fund-raising activity, as well:
- conduct a sales presentation,
- design an advertising campaign for the fund raiser,
- write a letter to possible sources of revenue explaining how the money from the campaign will be spent, and
- create a graph to track the progress towards the fund-raising goal.

While student involvement is encouraged in the planning and evaluation stages, caution should be taken when directly engaging children to raise funds. Procedural guidelines for student involvement should be approved by the school board and participation should be voluntary. It should be noted that the NAESP strongly believes students should not participate in door-to-door sales.

General Considerations and Cautions

Legal and ethical concerns are important issues in fund-raising. Determine procedures for how collected funds will be handled and secured. Specific accounting policies must also be established with records available to the public. It is recommended that two people be assigned to handle collected revenue. Both should be present when revenue is collected and calculators should be used to reduce error. Arrangements should be made to secure money at all times. In addition, attention should be given to protecting the identity of donors who wish to remain anonymous.

Safety Tips

- Parent and/or adult supervision should be required at all times.
- Focus fund-raising efforts on family and friends.
- Establish rules and procedures that are reviewed frequently both verbally and in writing to all those involved.

Getting Started: 10 Steps in Planning an Effective Creative Fund Raiser

Step 1: Get Permission

The first step in planning is to determine the local school board policies and local, state, and federal laws and regulations pertaining to fund-raising. Keep in mind that gathering necessary permissions may be time intensive, so start early.

Questions to Consider

- Are certain types of fund raisers, dates, and locations prohibited?
- Is personal and/or liability insurance necessary?
- Will sales tax be a consideration?
- Is parental permission for student participation required?

Step 2: Form a Committee and Name a Chairperson

A successful fund raiser requires the assistance of many hardworking and dedicated individuals. Teachers, administrators, parents, students, and others in the community can serve on the fund-raising committee. Groups should be kept to a manageable size and include those individuals with an interest in raising money. Once a committee has been formed, a chairperson should be appointed and other individual responsibilities designated. Be sure to select a chairperson who has the time necessary to devote to the project. In addition, keep in mind that a chairperson should possess:
- effective interpersonal skills,

- excellent communication skills,
- patience,
- dedication,
- proficient math skills,
- strong organizational skills,
- follow-through, and
- an eye for details.

Committees should meet regularly to plan and evaluate progress towards the established fund-raising goal.

Step 3: Set your Goal

Setting a realistic and specific goal is perhaps one of the most important steps in the fund-raising process. It is suggested that teachers, students, parents, administrators, and other interested parties be involved in the process of establishing fund-raising goals. Initial involvement will help everyone feel a sense of ownership and responsibility for the proposed project. In addition, the principal usually has a clear understanding of the school's overall fiscal situation and can identify areas of need. His or her endorsement of the fund-raising project may also help in obtaining commitment and support from other school personnel.

Questions to Consider

- What is the purpose of the fund raiser?
- Why is the money needed?
- How much money is needed?
- Who will benefit from the monies raised?
- What goal(s) will be accomplished by this fund raiser?

Step 4: Select an Idea

There are many fund-raising ideas from which to choose. Talk to other teachers, principals, PTO/PTA members, local organizations, and others to see what has worked for them. Tailor existing ideas to best meet the needs of your current situation and the interests of the community. Consider both the feasibility and potential profit, and select those ideas that are relatively easy to initiate and most profitable. The key is to think beyond the candy bars, wrapping paper, and bake sales (Stephens & Karnes, 1999). Commercial prepackaged events are always going to be available, but some of the most successful fund raisers can result from original ideas, so be creative! Appendix J contains a listing of some great ideas to explore.

Questions to Consider

- How profitable is the idea?
- How easy will this idea be to implement?
- Are the resources/materials available for ease of implementation?
- How successful has this idea been in the past?
- Will this idea appeal to the community?
- Is there another organization in the community using this idea or a similar one?

Step 5: Logistics: Determine Time and Place

Keep in mind that sales of particular types of products may be best suited for certain times of the year. For example, flowers may be most profitable around Valentine's Day and Mother's Day. Avoid planning your event at the same time of year as other schools and organizations in the community, for potential donors will become weary and you may not be able to raise as much money as hoped. Clear your selected dates with school officials (principals, coaches, custodians, board members) to avoid potential conflicts with other events that may be occurring.

Questions to Consider

- When are other fund-raising events currently scheduled in the school and community?
- Would this event be best suited for a particular holiday/season?
- How much planning time is needed before initiating the event or project?
- How much space is needed for the event?
- Is the space available for the selected dates and times?
- What should the duration of the event/project be?

Step 6: Make a Plan

Having a strategic fund-raising plan for your school that is updated annually is recommended. A school-wide plan helps communicate to others what types of fund raisers will be occurring and when, so appropriate decisions regarding new fund-raising initiatives can be made more effectively. Remember, it is better to have one or two fund raisers per year with 80 to 90% participation each time, than one event after another with only 30% participation.

The fund-raising committee should meet to develop the plan for the specific event. Suggested planning activities follow:

- make a list of necessary materials,
- determine the number of volunteers needed,
- develop a master schedule of important dates,
- assign designated tasks, and
- establish rules and procedures.

Additional areas to think about during the planning phase include:
- promotional materials,
- kickoff activities,
- deadlines for orders and money to be turned in,
- announcement of results,
- volunteer appreciation, and
- wrap-up meetings.

A helpful template for use in the planning process can be found in Appendix K (Fund-Raising Timeline).

Step 7: Recruit and Organize Volunteers

Volunteers are a vital element to fund-raising campaigns. While finding enthusiastic and committed volunteers can be frustrating, there are many things you can do to boost recruiting efforts and inspire participation.

Appoint someone to help secure volunteers. Select someone who is familiar with the community and has good interpersonal skills. It is important to secure enough volunteers to help ensure that the fund raiser will be successful.

Determine all tasks that need to be accomplished and write a job description for each. Be sure to include job responsibili-

Creative Fund Raising

ties, time commitment, and the skills that are necessary to perform required tasks.

Identify those individuals who might be interested in volunteering for your project/event. Keep in mind that parents are not the only source of volunteers. Others who are stakeholders in the school system should be considered, including community members, grandparents, teachers and other school personnel, local businesses, retirees, and others. Be sure to communicate up front with potential volunteers about what is expected of them and how much time they will be asked to devote to the project/event. This will help them determine if their involvement is feasible.

Screen and train your volunteers. Choose individuals who have a sincere interest in your efforts and will represent your organization in a positive manner. Most school districts now require a background check for volunteers, especially those who will be working in close contact with students. Make sure you are following school and district guidelines for screening potential volunteers. Once you have secured volunteers, it is essential that the goal of the fund-raising campaign be clearly communicated. Why is the money needed? For what purpose will the money be used? Who will benefit from the collected revenue? Volunteers must be able to answer all of these questions. In addition, they must be made aware of the specific procedures that are to be followed in soliciting and collecting revenue.

Encourage and involve your volunteers. Let the volunteers know how much their efforts are appreciated and provide encouragement along the way. Furthermore, get your volunteers involved immediately. No one wants to feel unneeded, so make sure there are always plenty of tasks available.

Celebrate and say thanks! In order to retain effective volunteers, it is necessary to provide appropriate recognition for their service. Awards, assemblies, articles with photos in the local newspaper, a special luncheon, and gift certificates are just a few examples of ways to show appreciation.

Plan for the future. Ask your volunteers to recommend others who may be interested in helping with future projects. If necessary, have them revise their job descriptions to better reflect the nature of the responsibility. It may be helpful to have them write out useful tips and suggestions pertaining to their tasks for others who may replace them in the future, especially if you intend on doing the same fund raiser for a number of years.

Wanted: Volunteers!

There are many methods for locating potential volunteers. For instance, at the beginning of the school year establish a parent talent bank. Collect information from parents about their interests and areas of expertise. Who knows, you may have a graphic artist, marketing director, or accountant in your midst. Put available talent to use. Job descriptions for needed volunteers can also be posted in the school newsletter or local newspaper, on a flyer sent home with students, or on a bulletin board located within the school.

Volunteers can:
- take care of publicity,

- handle money collection and record keeping,
- supervise students, and
- assist with organization and set-up

Questions to Consider:

- How many volunteers are needed to effectively carry out the project?
- How can I best utilize volunteers in the project?
- What skills must the volunteers have?
- Where within my community can I find volunteers?
- How will I thank the volunteers for their efforts?

Step 8: Target Potential Donors and Sponsors

The vast majority of money given away in the United States comes from individuals. Who are your stakeholders? Who would be most interested in supporting your project? Local businesses and school partnership participants are two places where potential donors and sponsors may be located. If several other school or community fund raisers are planned, steps should be taken to assure that the same individuals or donors are not targeted too frequently. The key to successful fund-raising is participation, so don't overextend your donors!

Some ideas for making contact with potential donors include:
- adding them to the school newsletter mailing,
- putting articles about your school/project in the local newspaper,
- extending special invitations to open house or other school events, and

- sending direct mail regarding your school and project/event.

Find out in what aspects of the school and its programs potential donors are interested. This information can be used for targeting them in future creative fund-raising endeavors. For example, Mr. Smith might be a retired librarian and is particularly interested in books for the school library. On the other hand, Mrs. Jones enjoys volunteering at the community animal shelter and would like to support civic and leadership programs for elementary school children to inspire future volunteerism. Ask potential donors what particular cause, program, or project they would like to support and keep records for future reference.

Step 9: Promote It

If you advertise, profit will come. If the community is unaware of your fund raiser, they can't contribute. Be sure to begin publicizing your fund raiser well in advance. There are a variety of methods that can be used to get the word out, including:
- banners,
- bulletin boards,
- flyers,
- intercom and radio announcements,
- newsletters,
- newspapers, and
- posters.

Other ideas might be to contact the local media and invite them to your kickoff, or get the mayor to sign a proclamation. For example, if the event is a book fair, the mayor might designate a special Day of Reading for the city. This is sure to generate some free publicity for your fund raiser.

Remember, money should be budgeted for marketing. Select those methods that have the potential to boost profit without breaking your budget. A sample media release and parent letter are included in Figures 5 and 6, respectively.

Step 10: Wrapping Things Up

Once the event or project is concluded, a comprehensive evaluation is strongly recommended. Questions on which to reflect include:
- Were financial expectations met?
- What improvements should be made for next year?
- Was the number of volunteers adequate?
- Were customers/donors satisfied?
- What was the minimum and maximum earned by fund-raising in the school district during the school year?

Dear Parent(s):

On September 9, 2006 at 1:00 p.m., Morristown High School will hold an Academic Bowl to help raise funds for a new science lab. The money raised will help fund the purchase of state-of-the-art laboratory equipment and instructional materials for the new lab.

The Academic Bowl is a fun and educational way for students, teachers, alumni, and community members to show support of this new initiative. Family and friends are welcome to support your child's participation through contributions. Checks should be made payable to the Morristown District Science Lab Fund.

We welcome your attendance at the event. We have many fun activities planned for the entire family.

If you have any questions or if you are interested in volunteering at the event, please contact me at 555-6543. We look forward to your participation in this very important effort.

Sincerely,

Mrs. Smith
Academic Bowl Coordinator

Figure 6. Sample letter to parents

Provide an overall evaluation report to the school administrator and determine how results of the fund raiser should be shared with the community and other stakeholders. All parents expect to receive an array of fund-raising materials at the beginning of school, but few anticipate the distribution of an annual report at the conclusion of the school year that summarizes the amount of money raised for each fund-raising event and how collected funds were used.

Recognition is perhaps one of the most important aspects of the fund raiser. Be sure to send thank-you letters to those individuals who volunteered their time to assist. For without their help, success would have not been possible. In addition, within the thank-you note, provide a listing of the items that will be purchased with the raised funds.

Some Creative and Successful Ideas to Share

Appendix J offers a broad listing of fund-raising ideas. While most of the ideas included are self-explanatory (or have been detailed in other publications), we have included a short list of 25 ideas with explanations. These were chosen for their feasibility and because they can be exciting ways to gather much needed funds. All of the ideas require student involvement, which helps promote school unity in fund-raising. Following these ideas, a few creative and successful fund raisers are shared by the teachers who implemented them. These teachers have described their event and provided tips in planning and practical advice for others considering similar ventures.

Bingo—Bingo is a fun, easy game that everyone can enjoy. Invite students, parents, teachers and other staff members, and the community to a Bingo night at the school. Charge an entrance fee or charge by the card, and be sure to have prizes for the winners. Refreshments can be sold for additional profit.

Bowling Night—Arrange a night of bowling with a local bowling alley, and ask for a discounted rate. You can charge an entrance fee per team, or have students and other participants obtain pledges from sponsors prior to the bowling night. Invite students and their families, as well as the community.

Calendars—Obtain (or have students take) pictures that highlight the events that have occurred during the school year. Be sure to include a variety of pictures that show various groups of students, teachers, classes, and organizations within the school. There must be enough variety included in the pictures to appeal to all students and their families. You may want to consider each classroom or organization sponsoring one page of the calendar and having a collage of pictures for each month instead of one picture featuring only one or two people.

Comedy Night—Schools have many talented students and teachers. Hold auditions for comedy night (in order to screen material), and sell tickets in advance and at the door. You might also want to invite a local comedian to headline the show if he or she is willing to donate the time. Comedy night can include stand up, as well as short funny skits.

Cookbook—Send out a call for students', parents', teachers', and other staff members' favorite recipes. Compile all of the recipes into a cookbook, have the book printed, and sell the books throughout the school year. Cookbooks should include recipes for appetizers, side dishes, salads, entrees, desserts, and so on, so be sure to gather a large number of recipes. Without a considerable response, people may not be as willing to buy a cookbook. Try to have your local copier give a discounted rate for printing a certain number of books, or ask the copier to donate a portion of the services.

Craft Fair—Designate a day for a craft fair. Crafts can be designed and made entirely by students, or you may want to invite parents, teachers, staff members, and community members to join in and sell their crafts at the fair, as well. Remind everyone that all proceeds will go toward the school fund raiser.

Debate Night—Students love a good debate. Organize a debate night, and have students (or teachers, staff members, and community members) debate controversial and interesting topics, especially those that apply directly to your school or community. Charge an entrance fee into the debate. This idea requires preparation on the part of the debate participants, as they will want to be prepared.

Dessert Night—Have people donate baked goods for a dessert night. It is best if people provide homemade desserts, as people might be willing to pay more for something that is homemade. Make sure people bring a wide variety of desserts—dessert night would not be as interesting if everyone brought chocolate chip cookies. Charge an entrance fee, or have people purchase the different desserts. You may want to also consider incorporating contests such as the best cake or best homemade ice cream. Provide prizes for the winners.

Dress-Down or Dress-Up Day—Designate one day each semester (or grading period) when students, teachers, and faculty members can purchase a ticket for Dress-Down or Dress-Up Day. Choose a price for a ticket that is reasonable (e.g., $1 for students, $3 for teachers). For schools that require uniforms, Dress-Down Day can be a day when everyone can wear jeans to school. Dress-Up Day could involve everyone purchasing a ticket to be able to dress up as their favorite storybook character or wear a crazy hat.

Faculty/Alumni Game or Faculty/Student Game—Have an annual faculty/alumni or faculty/student game for which everyone must purchase a ticket to attend. It is fun to invite the most recent alumni (e.g., recent high school graduates or students who moved up from junior high to high school) to participate in the game toward the beginning of the school year. Be sure to have an open call for all students interested in playing on the student team—don't just pick the members of the basketball team to play against the faculty in a basketball game.

Fall Festival—Prepare a festival for students, parents, teachers and staff members, and community members. This can be scheduled sometime after the beginning of the school year, but be sure to allow enough time to prepare for the festival. You might consider having different game booths sponsored by grade levels or organizations, a bake sale, and concessions.

Creative Fund Raising

If possible, try to have the food donated to save money. Rides or moonwalks are also fun ideas, but often cost quite a bit of money to secure. Consider having an entrance fee to the festival, or sell tickets to the different activities.

Game Night—Invite students, parents, teachers, and staff to bring their favorite games to game night. Organize which games will be brought in advance. You can schedule tournaments for popular games such as checkers, chess, and Monopoly, with the winners receiving prizes. Have an entrance fee, and consider selling refreshments.

Get Out of Class Ticket—Students can purchase tickets to get out of class for the last class period on a specified date. Have all students who purchased a ticket go to a set area to participate in an activity such as a popcorn party, movie, dance, or sporting event. Students should know the activity ahead of time so they can determine whether or not it is worth buying the ticket. Make the activity fun!

Guessing Game—Fill a jar with marbles or candy, and have students, teachers, and staff members purchase tickets to guess how many items are in the jar. The person closest to the actual number wins a prize.

Hat Day—Have students, teachers, and staff members purchase tickets for Hat Day, on which they can wear their favorite hat. You can tie it in to something that is being studied (e.g., Dr. Seuss hats if students are reading Dr. Seuss books), or hold a contest for the most creative hat, the craziest hat, and so on.

International Dinner Night—Organize an international dinner night, with a number of different entrees representing food from different countries. Students in different foreign language clubs may want to consider organizing this fund-raising event together. It is best to provide traditional foods from each country represented. Charge a fee for the dinner.

Karaoke Contest—Hold a karaoke singing contest at the school one afternoon or at night. Have the audience vote on the winner and provide the winner with a prize. Charge an entrance fee, and be sure to screen students before holding the contest. You might want to consider having an audition a few weeks prior to the scheduled event so students have time to practice their songs.

Penny Drive—Schedule a school-wide penny drive that will last over the course of a few weeks. Encourage students, parents, teachers, and staff members to collect and bring in pennies for the drive. Provide 5-gallon water bottles for each classroom or grade level so students can see the numbers of pennies grow over the course of the drive. Provide prizes for the winning classroom or grade level.

Play—Organize a grade level or school-wide play. Some schools designate the same grade level (e.g., sixth grade) to produce an annual school play, which may be picked from former Broadway plays or musicals. Have students try out for the parts and spend a few weeks rehearsing and preparing for the play. Have two showings: one for the school during the day and one for parents and family members at night. Charge a fee to get in to the play.

Creative Fund Raising

Read-A-Thon—Schedule a day of school-wide reading. Have students obtain pledges from sponsors (e.g., $1 a book), and be sure to have enough books readily available for each classroom. Define parameters—such as that picture books will not be considered a whole book for grades above kindergarten. Have parents donate snacks for the students, and try to keep children motivated during the entire Read-A-Thon by having contests for each grade level.

Rummage Sale—Organize a school-wide (or organization if large enough) rummage sale. Have students and parents donate slightly used items, with all proceeds going to the school. Be sure to advertise the rummage sale in the local paper or on the news so the community is aware that it is being held.

Tournament—Schedule a sports tournament for students, parents, teachers and staff members, and community members. This could include three-on-three basketball games, softball games, track and field activities, fun games (e.g., balloon toss), and so on. Charge an entrance fee, and make sure that the event has been well-organized prior to embarking on it.

T-shirt Sale—Have students design a T-shirt for the school (or grade level). You might want to consider having a T-shirt design contest, with the winner's design being made into the final T-shirt. Sell the T-shirts to students, parents, teachers, and staff members. Remember to take orders for the T-shirts prior to having them produced so you don't end up with the wrong sizes.

White Elephant Store—This is a good way for people to get rid of any White Elephant gifts they have sitting around the house. Have people donate their gifts and then set up a store for others to view and purchase the items.

Work for Donations—Have students, teachers, or staff members provide a service for donations. This could include walking pets, shoveling snow, raking leaves, mowing lawns, washing cars, and so on. It is of utmost importance to think of student safety at all times, so extreme caution should be taken with this fund-raising activity. Parental supervision is a must.

Fund-Raising Ideas From Teachers

Fund Raiser:	Parent's Night Out
Teacher:	Tommie Gail Bennett
Description:	We offered a babysitting service on a Friday night from 5–9 p.m. and charged $12 per child. The children had to bring a sack supper, which was eaten in the cafeteria after everyone arrived. We had games in the gym and watched a movie in the library. High school Beta Club members served as helpers to earn service hours. Prior to implementing the event, I got the school board's approval for liability protection.
Materials/Supplies:	TV, VCR or DVD player, video, games
Volunteers:	2 adults and 5–6 high school students, but more may be needed depending on the number of children attending.
Difficulty:	Easy
Profit:	Average $500–$600 per event (for only 4 hours of work!)
Advertising:	Flyers were sent home with the students prior to the event.
Advice:	Do not allow students below kindergarten age to attend, and be sure to have every minute planned to avoid behavior problems.

Fund Raiser:	Wall Painting
Teacher:	James Victor Davis, III
Description:	We have one wall made of large concrete stones in our building. Each year, we sell each block for $10 to the eighth graders at our school. Inside their purchased block, students may paint anything that they like (e.g., In Memory Of, their name, a picture, etc.). Some kids will combine their blocks to form a larger mural. Painting usually takes place on Saturday, and it is a lot of fun for the students. At the beginning of the next school year, we paint the wall white and sell the blocks again.
Materials/Supplies:	Paint, brushes, water, buckets, tarps, and paper towels
Volunteers:	3–4 adults
Difficulty:	Moderate
Profit:	Approximately $2,000 after purchasing materials
Advertising:	School newsletter, mailings, e-mails, and through the school news program
Advice:	Allow ample time for planning and preparation.

Fund Raiser:	Hot Dog Supper and Talent Show
Teacher:	James Victor Davis, III
Description:	We recently held a talent show, as well as a hot dog supper. The supper was inexpensive, easy to fix, and clean up was a snap. Tickets were sold for $5 each and included a hot dog, chips, a cookie, drink, and talent show admission. All food was donated for this event. The students chose to do a thematic talent show based on the movie *Grease*. We held the event at the school and the students did most of the work.
Materials/Supplies:	Stage, costumes, microphone, music equipment, props, paper plates, napkins, ice, and donated food
Volunteers:	At least 10 (stage lights, cooking, directing traffic, collecting money and tickets)
Difficulty:	Moderate
Profit:	Approximately $1,750 with the sale of 350 tickets
Advertising:	School newsletter, mailings, e-mails, and through the school news program
Advice:	Plan ahead! We were able to get the food donated to avoid extra expense, so it is more profitable to try to secure donated items. Local businesses and parents may be interested in donating food for the fund raiser.

Fund Raiser:	Art Show and Auction
Teacher:	Kim Taylor Davis
Description:	We conducted this fundraiser to enhance art resources for our K–5 art and music program. After studying different artists, each class designed artwork that represented the artist chosen by their class. The entire gym was transformed into a museum. The students created an invitation/brochure for their parents and the citizens of the community. Admission was free. The profit was made from the silent donations given when a person selected a piece of art. The students were honored to know that people other than their parents bought the art they created.
Materials/Supplies:	Basic art supplies
Volunteers:	The teacher and students. The students acted as the escorts and curators of the show. The teacher welcomed the public and accepted donations for the silent auction.
Difficulty:	Easy
Profit:	Approximately $350
Advertising:	Local newspaper, school signs, and student-made invitations
Advice:	Be flexible, allow students to be creative, and enjoy the night!

Fund Raiser:	Pansy Sales
Teacher:	Kirsten C. Muldoon
Description:	Students used coupons to sell flats of pansies. The coupons contained two sections: one part for the customer to retain and the other for the student to keep for order processing. Coupons indicate the color flower selected, number of flats ordered, and delivery date and pick-up location. Orders were taken 6 weeks before delivery, and money was collected at the time the order was placed. On the designated day, customers picked up their flowers at the school. Different types of flowers can be sold depending on the season.
Materials/Supplies:	Printed coupon books, flowers
Volunteers:	3 adults (parents)
Difficulty:	Moderate
Profit:	Approximately $3,000
Advertising:	PTA newsletter
Advice:	Keep in mind that for fall sales, flowers must be ordered from the grower in June/July.

Fund Raiser:	Holiday Store
Teacher:	Sylvia Anderson
Description:	The classroom was arranged to resemble a store, and tables are covered with festive tablecloths. Each table holds specifically priced items (e.g., 25¢, 50¢, $1, $2, etc.). Children from various classes walk through, select their items, and go to the cashier's line. Students could also purchase decorative bags for 25¢ in which the gifts could be placed. Items were donated, made by students, or ordered through Oriental Trading Company.
Materials/Supplies:	Merchandise, posters, bags, cashier's box
Volunteers:	2 teachers and 10 students
Difficulty:	Moderate
Profit:	Approximately $700
Advertising:	Posters made by students, announcements on the school intercom.
Advice:	Start preparing for the holiday store in early October.

Fund Raiser:	Anniversary Afghan
Teacher:	Jenny Vanderford
Description:	Pictures were collected of various stages of our school's history, grade level activities, or yearly events. The photographs were placed in a selected design on poster board. For example, larger photos were placed in the middle and corners, and a border can be sketched as desired. The design was submitted to Loom Craft [P.O. Box 825, Belton, SC 29627; (864) 338-3064; http://www.loomcraftinc.com] along with the payment, which was approximately $125. It took approximately 4–6 weeks for them to send the afghan. We displayed the afghan and took orders. For our sale, our cost was $27.00 per afghan, so we sold each afghan for $45.00, thus making a small profit per afghan.
Materials/Supplies:	Photos and/or drawings of events or symbols, poster board
Volunteers:	5–6
Difficulty:	Moderate
Profit:	Approximately $4000
Advertising:	Posters and banners
Advice:	Choose people to be on the design team who work well together.

Fund Raiser:	Celebrity Raffle
Teacher:	LaGatha Kay
Description:	My students wrote letters to their favorite celebrity and/or sports figure asking for miscellaneous articles like autographed pictures to be donated to help raise funds for a specific purpose (i.e., a field trip). These items were then raffled to help raise money for the class. Raffle tables were set up at local sporting events, and the raffle winners were photographed for publication in the local newspaper.
Materials/Supplies:	Computer, Internet access, raffle ticket, paper, envelopes, and postage
Volunteers:	5–35, depending on the size of the raffle
Difficulty:	Moderate
Profit:	Approximately $500
Advertising:	Posters, newspaper, school intercom
Advice:	Start early to make contact with celebrities, as some may not respond. Students might also want to consider including local celebrities, who may be more likely and willing to participate in the raffle by donating an item.

Fund Raiser:	Theme Baskets
Teacher:	Lina Soares
Description:	Teachers and students determined themes for each basket and generated a list of possible items to include in each basket according to the designated theme. Students from participating classes brought in donated items from the list to include in the baskets. As items are secured, the teacher, students, and/or volunteers arranged the articles in wicker baskets. The baskets were raffled off with raffle tickets at a cost of $1 each.
Materials/Supplies:	5–6 large wicker laundry baskets, items to fill the basket according to the themes
Volunteers:	One per classroom
Difficulty:	Moderate
Profit:	Approximately $10,000 (with raffle ticket sales)
Advertising:	Flyers, intercom announcements, joined with PTSA
Advice:	The baskets could be offered in a silent auction instead of a raffle. If you are having trouble securing donated items from students, you may want to consider contacting local businesses for possible donations.

Fund Raiser:	Dinner Theater
Teacher:	Glenn Nobles
Description:	Students prepared a performance of a medley of Disney tunes (other selected songs/performances could be prepared instead). Arrangements were made for a caterer to serve a buffet-style meal at the event. Teachers and students sold printed tickets for $10 each approximately 2 weeks before the scheduled show.
Materials/Supplies:	Auditorium or community center, tables and chairs, sound equipment, food, decorations, tickets
Volunteers:	15 adults
Difficulty:	Moderate
Profit:	Approximately $1,500 (after catering expenses)
Advertising:	Local newspaper, public broadcasting television
Advice:	Find a caterer who will give you a price per plate that is $5.00 or less. It is helpful to have a lot of volunteers involved.

Fund Raiser:	Flamingo Yard Decorations
Teacher:	Jennifer Blackwood
Description:	Individuals paid $25 for the group of students to decorate a certain person's yard. The group decorated the designated yard one night with flamingos and a sign that said, "Somebody at <insert school name> loves you!" or "You helped raise money for <insert name of school>!" The decorations remained in the person's yard for one day. If the person wanted them removed immediately, the students charged the individual to have the decorations taken off of the yard, which helped raise more money. Flamingo insurance was also offered to an individual after his or her yard has been decorated in order to ensure that no more flamingos would be placed there in the future. If a yard was large, a double flamingo decoration was provided for a higher price.
Materials/Supplies:	25–30 pink flamingos, sign
Volunteers:	10–15
Difficulty:	Easy
Profit:	Average, depending on the number of individuals willing to pay for decorating
Advertising:	Newsletter, newspaper, school and district Web site

Advice: This fund raiser has to be approached very carefully. Students must be considerate of the fact that some people do not want their yards decorated, even if it is for a good cause.

Fund Raiser:	Great Storytelling
Teacher:	Bernice Franklin
Description:	Students wrote an elementary level version of a book they have read. The student stories were then compiled into one book and sold during an open house and other schoolwide events. To help increase interest, a storytelling room was set up and students were able to rotate reading their stories to interested listeners. We charged admission to get into the "story room" and sold inexpensive refreshments inside to raise more funds.
Materials/Supplies:	Writing supplies, copier, binding materials
Volunteers:	Students and 3–6 adults
Difficulty:	Moderate
Profit:	Average, depending on the costs involved in printing the book
Advertising:	Newsletter, newspaper, school and district Web site
Advice:	Plan thoroughly and make sure the students have enough time to prepare quality stories prior to the event.

Fran Woodworth:
The Campbell's Soup Label Lady

Fran Woodworth is a secretary at Red Bird, a United Methodist school and mission in southeastern Kentucky. Red Bird began collecting labels through the Campbell's Soup Labels for Education program in 1983. As a result, they have received 7 minivans and 16 passenger vans, as well as a wide variety of school supplies.

Below, Fran responds to some questions pertaining to her phenomenal efforts with the label program.

How did you become involved in the label program?

Have you ever known any school that has had enough resources? Our school joined the label program as soon as we heard about it in 1983. In addition to the labels collected from our school's staff and families, members and friends of the United Methodist Church across the country began to send us their labels. We received our first Campbell's van in 1990 and have been able to order at least one new van every year since that time.

How do you facilitate the collection of labels?

Recognizing all the individuals who help us by saving labels is a very important part of this program. When labels arrive in the office, the name and address of the giver is immediately recorded. Thank-you receipts are sent for label gifts, both large and small. The labels are then quickly sorted (we try to keep up with it each day, sometimes we don't get

Please fill out the following information and include with your next shipment!

Name: _____

Address: _____

City, State, Zip: _____

Optional Information: _____

Campbell's Labels Qty:___ General Mills Box Tops Qty:___
Tyson A+ Qty:___

Return to:
School Name
Address
City, State, Zip

Figure 7. Sample label form

it done) into two categories: 1) uncut or unprocessed labels and 2) labels that are cut and/or counted. We have one volunteer who becomes responsible for the labels at this point, and other staff members and volunteers help as needed. Sometimes the school children will be learning "sets" and so counting by 10s, 100s, and 500s is helpful as a learning tool. Involving the children in the collecting of the labels and letting them know when something they are using was purchased with Campbell's labels is important.

We have developed a special form (see Figure 7), which can be included when an individual sends us his/her collected labels. Many of our donors enjoy keeping track of how many labels they have contributed. Sometimes we have contests between classes or between teachers and students. The form also gives us a quick way to get out a thank-you letter with another form to include in their next gift.

When the catalog, with all the items that can be purchased with labels, arrives from Campbell's, we create a "what-to-save" packet. We include a list of participating products and directions on how to cut and bundle labels. A listing of all the things we have purchased with labels in the past and our wish list for the upcoming year is also included in the packet.

If we get behind, because of weather or a very high volume of labels, we schedule a soup supper. It starts right after school and continues until 7 p.m. Everyone is invited to bring their scissors; eat a bowl of soup, salad, and dessert; and cut, count, and tie labels. One time we were able to process about 26,000 labels in a 3-hour period!

We have a collection barrel at school and in each of the mission areas. We try to make it easy to drop off labels. Visitors to our campus get a tour of our school and the mission facilities. That tour always includes the label room. Seeing more than 1 million labels is eye opening. When we talk about the labels, we emphasize that someone may not be able to give large financial gifts to support our school, but everyone eats or cooks with soup, and individual label gifts can add up to great resources for our school. Every newsletter, every meeting, every time folks get together, they are reminded to save and bring their soup labels.

How many volunteers are needed?

It is important to have one person who is in charge of the project. Our principal gets all the mail from Campbell's and is our official person. Beyond that, any number of volunteers can be utilized.

Creative Fund Raising

What are the benefits of the program?

The number one benefit of the label program is the ability to purchase/redeem labels for items we would not otherwise be able to have. Our executive director estimates that we have collected and redeemed more than 25 million labels since 1983. If a school or school district collected labels, they would redeem those labels at a value of just under 2 cents each—with little or no money spent for the items acquired.

What advice would you give others considering this type of program?

A program like this takes just a few committed people to get it started. It might get off to a slow start, but do not get discouraged. Regular reminders such as, "Yes, we still collect labels, boxtops, etc." are important. It is also essential to find a way to say thank you to those individuals or groups who help with the project (e.g., class of the month, individual who worked overtime for the program, etc.). In addition, it is vital to keep up with the project each week. Do not wait until the last minute to count and organize your labels for shipment.

The Campbell's company has been generous to schools with this program. I understand that Campbell's recycles all the labels they receive. Isn't that great?

Additional Tidbits

Internet Fund-Raising

Will Internet fund-raising become the wave of the

future? This new way of fund-raising has taken on many forms. For example, some companies like Schoolpop.com (http://www.schoolpop.com), which has joined forces with Schoolcash.com, and SchoolMall.com (http://www. schoolmall.com), allow schools to receive a percentage of the purchases generated from online shopping at popular stores. At this time, experts say that this new wave of fund-raising should be a supplement rather than a replacement to more traditional forms of fund-raising. The Washington Post (Trejos, 2000) recently reported that one of the largest companies in Internet fund-raising boasts a customer base of 17,000 schools netting only $1 million for an average of $53 per school. However, as more consumers resort to online shopping, this form of fund-raising can be expected to grow.

Although few principals (8%) in the NAESP (2000) survey indicated an involvement with fund-raising on the Internet, there are some advantages and disadvantages to this form of acquiring monies. According to Mabry (2000), it is less labor intensive than other creative fund-raising activities with fewer volunteers needed. In addition, a smaller quantity of printed materials may be required, which helps keep costs down. Online fund-raising also allows flexibility for individuals to make purchases at any time during the day (or night). On the other hand, sales could be somewhat limited due to the fact that not everyone has Internet access. Though this form of fund-raising is still quite young, the market is already becoming crowded.

When contacting an Internet fund-raising company there are several questions that should be asked:

- What is the rebate being offered? What percentage of the profits does the school receive?

Creative Fund Raising

- Is there a minimum amount that must be reached before a check is issued?
- What happens if the minimum is not reached?
- What is the company's privacy policy?
- In what ways are customer service representatives available to provide assistance?
- Who are some of the company's current customers and are references available?

Selecting the Right Product or Company

If you select to work with a fund-raising company, there are several things to keep in mind. Do not hesitate to ask for and check out references. Select a company with a successful track record that offers quality products at fair prices. Let the company know your financial goal, the number of expected participants and their ages, and any other relevant information. Look for signs of good communication and customer service, and be sure to obtain a written agreement so a clear understanding of the proposal is established and your organization is protected.

Other questions to ask potential companies include:
- How long has the company been in business?
- How responsive is the company when problems arise?
- What services are available?
- Are products paid for in advance or upon delivery?
- Does the company comply with state tax laws?
- What promotional assistance does the company provide?
- Are samples of their product(s) available?

- How are products shipped and who pays for it?
- What form of record-keeping is used to track orders?
- What is the return policy?
- What is their policy pertaining to back-ordered items or if an item becomes unavailable?

Kickoffs

A kickoff is the day the sale or event is to begin. Statistics show that schools choosing to have a kickoff will generate a higher profit than those who do not. In addition, kickoffs provide a unified sense of purpose and participation among the students, teachers, parents, and volunteers. Typically, a kickoff consists of a school assembly where possible incentives for participation are revealed. Other ideas for kickoffs include:
- balloon launches,
- banquets or picnics,
- special guest appearances,
- special button or ribbon days,
- "a-thons,"
- tournaments,
- raffles, and
- parties.

Incentive Programs

Stickers, movie passes, rulers, pencils, books, puzzles, educational software, and more are used every day to motivate individuals to take an active role in the fund-raising event. The ultimate goal is to get students, parents, and the community to *want* to help the school. However, some worry that expensive item incentives may overexcite students and place undue pressure and stress on them to compete with each other. Others feel that in an effort to "win," children may be tempted to ignore rules and not follow appropriate procedures. Despite these negatives, offering incentives does nearly double participation. The key is to focus on *effort* rather than *greed*. Some innovative incentive ideas follow.

- Money raised by a particular classroom goes to that classroom, rather than equally splitting the profit among all classes in a grade level.
- Offer a teacher incentive for a class that achieves 100% participation (e.g., educational software and materials).
- Have a tiered system where awards are given at different levels based on sales achievement. You can recognize individual, classroom, and school-wide participation.
- Tie incentives to other creative fund-raising projects in the school (e.g., free admission to the school carnival and athletic events or merchandise at the student store).
- Move from child-centered to a classroom-centered incentive program (e.g., provide popcorn, pizza, after-school field trips, movie day, or ice cream parties to the class with the most participation).
- Have an equitable raffle system. Every student who participates, no matter what level, receives a raffle ticket. The individuals whose tickets are drawn receive awards.

Questions of Caution:

- Are the prizes excessive, detracting from your organization's mission or fund-raising purpose?
- Will the incentive encourage excessive competition so that inappropriate or unsafe selling will occur?

Sales Tax

An online resource to assist in answering state sales tax questions is located at http://www.fundraisetaxlaw. org. Information from this site was compiled from a survey of the revenue departments of 38 states and the District of Columbia. At this Web site, you will be able to find the answers to a number of questions, including:

- What types of groups are exempted from fund-raising sales tax?
- Are there certain types of products that are exempted from sales tax?
- Are there state limitations on exemptions?
- Who is responsible for collecting and remitting the tax?
- What is the basis for calculating sales tax?

Keep in mind that laws in this area often change, so maintain up-to-date records as you plan your next fund raiser.

Final Words of Inspiration

Once your fund-raising year has concluded, it is almost time to once again start planning for future ones. To assure a smooth transition into your next venture, it will be helpful if

Creative Fund Raising

you continue to build your volunteer pool, keep good notes to pass on to the next fund-raising chair, and create a fund-raising timeline that includes as many details as possible. For example:

- When should a creative fund-raising committee be formed?
- At what point should an idea be selected?
- When should we start promoting the event/project?

Whatever your endeavor, good luck and have fun!

Part IV

Fund Development

In addition to creative fund-raising and grants, fund development is becoming another way to secure monies for schools. Allen (1998) urged elementary and secondary schools to follow the lead traditionally set by colleges and universities. There are several levels involved in fund development: annual giving, planned giving, capital campaigns, endowments, and foundations. Each level requires planning, attention to detail, an identified donor base, detailed record keeping, trained volunteers, and other necessary elements.

Donor Research

Before engaging in any type of fund development, it is important to assess who your donors will be. Who will be asked to support your school or district? What will they support? What amount would be suggested based on their interest and capability? How you answer these questions and where such information is located are other important factors to consider.

Researching donors is an ongoing but necessary process to all aspects of fund development. The first step is to assemble background information on prospective and current donors both inside and outside of the district. Determine the nature of the questions to be asked. Research policies need to be formulated and approved. Imbedded in the written and approved document should be statements on data storage and retrieval. Access to the donor database should only be given to certain individuals, as many donors wish to remain anonymous. Confidentiality and ethics must be held at the highest level. The Association of Professional Researchers for Advancement (APRA) and the National Society of Fund Raising Executives (NSFRE) have statements on such ethics. These can be used as guidelines for developing and implementing related policies. Appendix R (Donor Identification Form) provides a useful of way of recording and saving information related to perspective donors.

Where Do You Find Donors?

Information on potential donors is available from a wide variety of sources within the community. Again, all individuals involved with the school should be considered for annual giving and/or a Family Support Campaign (see p. 87). There will be people with special interests in youth and their educational needs who will want the opportunity to do more for your school or district. Newspapers and magazine articles can be sources of information and can illustrate the history of donors' community contributions. Tax records could also be valuable sources of information. Annual reports from local agencies and sponsor listings can provide the names of donors and in some cases, their levels of giving.

Potential Donors Community General Listing	Potential Donors In-School General Listing
• Parents	• Teachers/Teacher Aids
• Grandparents	
• Other family members	• Principals/Assistant Principals
• Business	• Psychologists
• Fine and Performing Arts	• Counselors
• Media	• Librarians
• Sports/Leisure	• Custodians
• Medicine	• Nurses
• Law	• Office Managers/Clerks
• Clergy	• Media Specialists

Sources of information beyond the community are also available. IRS records, available through the Foundation Center with affiliate libraries across the country, yield great information on potential donors. Published reference books by profession, industry, prominence, and so forth are also additional sources.

How Do You Get Donor Support?

To build strong donor support, it is vital to develop prospective relationships with each donor based on interest, involvement, information, and invitation. People will give funds to help support something that is of personal interest to them in the school or district. For example, supporters of the arts will give to the visual and/or performing arts. For those who identify with sciences and/or mathematics, their gifts will be directed to those areas. Determining the interest of potential donors will assist in focusing on the area(s) of funding important to them.

Getting people involved in their area(s) of interest will further enhance their potential for giving. This can be accomplished by providing information to them in a variety of forms. Newsletters, annual reports, brochures, flyers, programs, e-mail messages, or telephone calls are but a few examples of ways to share information with potential donors.

Invitations to events and activities focusing on their interest will further the communication lines. People like to see students perform and display their abilities through the school or district. Direct involvement strengthens interest and enhances the prospect of potential or continuing donors.

How Do You Thank Donors?

Paramount to relationship building is to acknowledge donor participation and giving. Some form of recognition must be given to all who contribute. However, there are always a few donors who wish to remain anonymous. That wish must be honored at all times. To those donors, sending letters, giving plaques, and other forms of recognition must remain private.

For those donors who do not prefer anonymity, there are many ways to recognize their generosity. A thank-you note or letter is a must at all levels of giving. When the contribution is tied to a particular group of students, donors respond very well to letters, posters, or artwork from the students.

However, the last names of youth should not be given to ensure confidentiality. Other forms of recognition, depending on the level of giving, could be certificates, plaques, paperweights, crystal bowls, or silver trays/bowls.

Annual Giving

Annual giving involves the raising of private funds each year by telephone and/or direct mail solicitation (Greenfield, 1994). Families of current students, alumni, and friends of the school or district are asked to give money for specific or general purposes. For small groups of perspective donors, annual giving can be conducted through individual meetings. For each large targeted group, phone banks should be established, accurate lists of persons to call maintained, and individuals trained to make the calls. In addition, accurate record keeping from year to year must be kept in order to make this type of fund-raising successful. Usually thank-you letters are immediately forwarded to those responding by phone in a favorable manner, reminding them of the amount they agreed to pledge, with a return self-addressed stamped envelope for their contributions. Although this is time consuming and not as productive in terms of large dollar amounts, it can produce a stream of revenue and serve as the foundation for larger gifts in the future. Mail solicitation without telephone calls will not typically yield the same results.

Another idea for annual giving is a Family Support Campaign. This campaign is based on the concept that each family is capable of giving at some level. Acknowledging that almost every school and community family gives to the school district by paying taxes, parents, grandparents, aunts, uncles, brothers, and sisters need to support the fund development effort based on the needs of the school district. Broadening the concept of families to all school personnel will send a powerful message, and the focus on family will greatly enhance the giving power.

Tips for Planning an Annual Giving Campaign

A committee should be formed, a timetable established, and a budget constructed when commencing an annual giving campaign. The necessary expenditures must be weighed against the potential profit. In addition, there are several questions to be asked before annual giving or a Family Support Campaign can be operational. Here are a few to consider:

- Who will manage the campaign?
- How many volunteers will be needed?
- How will their roles be defined?
- Is training needed and, if so, who will do it?
- What logistics need to be discussed and planned?

Annual giving campaigns can be facilitated through direct mail, phone-a-thons, PTA/PTO meetings, open houses, and other events.

Direct Mail: The Solicitation Letter

Direct mail solicitation usually yields somewhat lower donations. Keys to successful mail campaigns rely on several pivotal items, including the solicitation letter. Writing an effective fund-raising letter is extremely important. According to Lewis (1989), there are many helpful rules to consider. A few of his ideas are on the overall appearance of the letter. For instance:

- Ragged right indentions are more personal than flush right ones;
- paragraphs should be no longer than seven lines;
- active voice is better than passive;
- a letter with a "P.S." at the end is more effective than one without;
- letters should be limited to one page;
- use underlining or italics sparingly, because all will have equal weight;
- contractions (e.g., I've, Let's, You're) are more cordial than those spelled out;
- using a typewriter face makes the letter have more appeal than fancy print;
- bullets should not be used, as they damage the effect of urgency;
- messages must be clear. Clarity is the hallmark of a great fund-raising letter;
- use a cordial greeting such as "Good morning" or "Dear Friend";
- the word "you" is powerful when making appeals for funding, but do not use "those of you";
- avoid acronyms or "educationalese" that people may find confusing; and
- "we need your assistance/help" is overused and not very effective.

Having a specific time of the year to send a letter for annual giving is helpful. Always give the reader an exact date for receiving the contribution and, if the organization is nonprofit, remind them their donation is tax-deductible. Enclose a self-addressed stamped envelope to guarantee a higher rate of return. A sample fund-raising letter is included in Figure 8.

Capital Campaigns

Strategies to secure large amounts of money in a specified time frame is the primary purpose in a capital campaign (Kihlstedt & Schwartz, 1997). Potential donors are identified and money is secured through major gifts and pledges. The success of such an endeavor involves thorough planning and preparation, which is based on strategic and long-term goals. The needs of the district must parallel the goal(s) of the capital campaign. The justification for the financial need(s) will assist the donors in being more willing to provide financial support. A strategic plan based on school/community input should form the basis of the capital campaign. Once, capital campaigns were designated only for buildings, new facilities, equipment, or renovations. However, currently included in such campaigns are endowments, needed scholarships, and physical and operating needs.

The donor base must be determined with the realization that nearly 80% of the funding in a capital campaign comes from only about 20% of the donors. Such an initiative usually begins with a silent phase during which time major gifts are obtained from individuals, foundations, corporations, and other entities. The capital campaign becomes public when approximately 70% of the goal has been reached.

The emphasis is then shifted in the public phase to individuals and organizations with lesser financial potential. Extensive public relations, including print and non-print materials, solicitations, and presentations can be utilized

Dear John Q. Public:

Your help is needed to advance the children in our school district. The Quincy Educational Foundation has been established to support our public schools based on identified needs. As a former student, you know the quality educational opportunities you received. With cuts in the state education budget, all of us need to support our schools.

The following are critical to the learning of our students:

> instructional software
> library materials
> science equipment

Your tax-free donation of $100 by March 10 will greatly assist in the budgeting of these needs for the next school year. The self-addressed stamped envelope is enclosed for your convenience.

Thank you for supporting the educational needs of our children.

Sincerely yours,

John Chambliss, President
The Quincy Educational Foundation

Figure 8. Sample fund-raising letter

when seeking smaller gifts. The donors of major gifts, unless they want to remain anonymous, should be recognized during the public phase of the capital campaign. Major gift donors may wish to be involved in the public phase through solicitation and statements of support. Progress on both the silent and public phases should be consistently monitored with a well-developed evaluation plan.

Celebration is in order when the goal of the capital campaign has been reached through dollars and pledges. A celebration is an opportunity to recognize all the donors, volunteers, and staff who have made the capital campaign a success. Be sure to include everyone who has assisted in the campaign, no matter how small their role. Such an event also needs to be well planned and publicized.

The last step is the overall evaluation of this major fundraising endeavor. These questions may serve as a beginning to the evaluation process:

- What strategies worked and why?
- Which ones should be avoided in the future and why?
- Which constituencies exceeded their estimated potential and which fell short?
- Which volunteers were successful?
- What lessons were learned?
- Can these lessons be applied to strengthen future campaigns?

Not all capital campaigns are successful. An unsuccessful one also needs to be examined and evaluated, as it can be damaging to the image of the school. Public knowledge of a failure may dampen donors' willingness to invest in other fund-raising activities. Also, it could curb the willingness of volunteers to continue to participate in other giving activities. Not meeting the goal will also put a drain on the financial resources of the district with ramifications for years to come.

The reward of a successful capital campaign, in addition to having a large funding base, is a new group of donors. They have the potential of providing additional donations when needed. Also, additional volunteers who know how to identify, cultivate, and solicit donors have been secured. Another plus of a successful capital campaign is the establishment or expansion of your donor database.

Readiness for a Capital Campaign

There are several major principles on which to build a capital campaign. The best donors are usually those who have already given to your district. Have they been cultivated and thanked for what they have contributed in the past? Do you know enough about them and other possible major gift donors to create customized approaches that will increase the likelihood of them giving again?

Another major principle is "Top down, inside out." In translation, this means that the largest gifts are solicited first. You start with those who are most closely associated with the school or those who have a vested interest in the school or district. A major gift plan should be developed after a careful analysis of the top potential donors.

This type of plan indicates a top gift of 10–20% of the goal, two gifts of 5–10% of needed monies, four to six gifts at 5% of the goal, and so on. It is helpful in determining the number of prospects and volunteers needed to achieve the designated amount.

Other Giving Opportunities

Cash to school districts is a simplistic form of giving. If the donor itemizes deductions, the full market value of a cash gift is deductible at up to 50% of the donor's adjusted gross income. Excess contributions can be carried over the next 5-year period.

Appreciated security is an additional way to support education and to get a tax deduction. Donating stocks that have gained in worth will give the donor a tax deduction of the full fair market value if the person owned them for a year or more. For example, if a donor purchased 100 shares of stock at $5 and the value increase to $10, upon donating the stock, he or she could claim a federal tax deduction of $1,000.

Real estate can also be a donated. The fair market price based on an appraisal by a licensed appraiser can be used as a tax deduction. Income from rental property can be handled in the same manner. Tangible personal property can also be a tax deduction for the donor. Pieces of art, books, computers, and audio-visual equipment are a few examples of tangible personal property. Again, the donor must have the fair market value to determine the tax deduction. It must be kept in mind that the school district has the right of refusal.

Planned Giving

Those who want to help provide for the future of education may include in their financial plans a program of charitable giving (White, 1995). Individuals give because they believe in the potential of education. With careful planning, they may also receive a tax advantage for their donation. In addition, the donor who makes a planned gift today provides money and resources for the education of tomorrow's students.

Basically, there are two types of planned gifts: *irrevocable charitable gifts* and *revocable charitable gifts*. Irrevocable charitable gifts are absolute, meaning they cannot be withdrawn or changed once the gift has been donated. On the other hand, revocable charitable gifts are those the donors may choose to alter or terminate during their lifetime. Furthermore, irrevocable gifts provide instant tax deductions for the donor, while revocable charitable gifts provide a potential estate tax deduction at the time of the donor's death.

Forms of Planned Giving

Other forms of planned giving include life insurance policies, bequests, a Pooled Income Fund, a Charitable Remainder Trust, and retirement plan assets. These types of donations allow a donor to give a much larger donation than would be possible with an outright gift, thus enabling the donor to maximize their tax benefits.

Life Insurance Policy—A life insurance policy, whether new or existing, designated to a school or Local Education Fund (LEF) as the beneficiary, is deductible for estate tax purposes. Upon the death of the donor, the value of the life insurance policy would go to the school or LEF. Also, schools or other organizations could be named as a contingent beneficiary. This means that if the primary beneficiary dies before the policyholder, the proceeds would go to another designated group (the contingent beneficiary).

Bequests/Wills—Bequests are another way of giving money through a will. Cash gifts and/or property designated in a will can be used to reduce estate and inheritance taxes.

The bequest should name an exact amount or item to be given for either a general or specific purpose.

Pooled Income Fund—A Pooled Income Fund allows the donor to make an irrevocable gift that can be pooled with other high quality investment producing income. A federal tax deduction can be taken at the time of the donation and donors receive quarterly income payments for life from the Fund according to the amount given.

Charitable Remainder Trust—A Charitable Remainder Trust gives the donor the opportunity to have a lifetime deduction or up to 20 years of income and a charitable income tax deduction. A pay-out rate of at least 5% is selected by the donor. In some situations, this type of donation could provide the donor with a supplemental income.

There are two types of Charitable Remainder Trusts: annuity and unitrust. The annuity trust pays a fixed dollar income regardless of the investment performance of the trust. The income rate is established at the time the trust is funded. The unitrust yields a predetermined percent of the fair market value of the assets of the trust as determined annually. If the trust assets increase, a larger payment is received. Additional contributions can be made to a unitrust.

Charitable Lead Trust—A Charitable Lead Trust involves the transferring of cash, securities, privately held stocks, real estate, or limited partnerships. The donor receives either a fixed dollar amount or a fixed percentage of the Trust principal, as determined annually. At the end of the Trust agreement, the principal is distributed to the donor's designated beneficiaries.

Fund Development

Retirement Plans—Retirement plan assets can be doubly taxed. Potential donors should be made aware of this possibility. If the remainder of a retirement plan is given to a charity, most taxes to the heirs will be avoided. As with most giving plans, a lawyer should advise both the donor and the recipient of all possible benefits.

Endowments—Although endowments to public school education are a relatively new approach to funding local programs, they do provide a steady income based on the interest earned off the capital. Endowments are usually large gifts given by private individuals or groups and, when invested wisely, will yield interest to use as specified by the donor. Endowments are usually sizeable amounts of money. Ten thousand to millions of dollars are usually given for endowments to public schools. A conservative investment of a $10,000 endowment at 5% interest would annually yield $500. A $1 million endowment at the same interest rate would render $50,000.

Endowments can be established for almost any worthwhile purpose. Some purposes may include scholarships for teachers, principals, and/or students to participate in designated workshops, travel experiences, or other learning opportunities. An endowment could be designated to purchase original pieces of art on an annual basis for a school or for equipment for a robotics course or other science programs. When the donor sees the benefits of the endowment, he or she is more likely to continue to contribute.

As with all dimensions of planned giving, the donor will determine if they wish to remain anonymous. Endowments may bear the name of the donor or of a loved one to be honored or remembered. With or without public recognition, the donor must always be thanked in a proper manner.

Local Educational Funds

Local Education Funds (LEFs) are changing the way education is funded in the United States. They differ from one location to another as to their activities, but their central purpose is the improvement of public education within a specific geographic area, specifically in low-income communities. This means that revenues must be generated to support local educational needs. The Public Education Network (PEN), a group of local school reform organizations, indicates that millions of dollars have been generated to support elementary and secondary education through LEFs.

How Do You Start a LEF?

There are several routes to starting a LEF, but the following ideas have been used by most and have proven to be successful. Before launching into the establishment of a LEF, learn about other such organizations. Determine what advice they would give in building a new LEF, and learn from the successes and mistakes of other groups. For more information about LEFs, please visit Public Education Network's Web site (http://www.publiceducation.org/lefs.asp).

The recruitment of a steering committee comprised of local leaders is also necessary. Ten or 12 people interested in supporting local education is a good starting point. An explanation of how other LEFs are organized and their purposes should be given to the committee. Written materials from successful LEFs would also be helpful. The steering committee should formulate the purpose(s) of the LEF and design a plan of action.

Share the LEF's goals and plan with the superintendent and members of the local school board. They must see the value of establishing a LEF and how the support generated can be used for the advancement of students, teachers, and other school personnel. It should be made clear that the proposed LEF will not conflict with the duties and roles of the school board members and the superintendent. It should be emphasized that the LEF is being established to support the needs of education at the local level.

With approval of the local school board, schedule a meeting with those in the community who wish to learn more about the proposed goals and plan for the establishment of a LEF. Input from citizens will strengthen community support and provide additional ideas on which to build the organization.

The steering committee should create the bylaws and constitution. The constitution will establish the structure and format of the LEF, while the bylaws will detail the process and procedures needed to implement the proposed structure. The constitution should include items such as:

- the name of the LEF;
- the purpose of the LEF;
- qualifications of board members and officers, when elections will typically occur, the title of each office and a brief description of duties;
- the frequency of meetings and how they are scheduled and participants notified;
- guidelines for the decision-making process (e.g., how many participants must be present to conduct business);
- the number of votes needed to amend the constitution; and
- procedures for disbursal of assets if the LEF should cease to exist.

Bylaws should contain information relating to:

- the location of the LEF's offices;
- the number of directors constituting the Board of Directors, the length of their term, and specified qualifications to serve;
- the procedures regarding the election and removal of board members;
- the schedule and procedures for board meetings;
- a description of the officers of the LEF with details pertaining to their election, term, compensation, removal, and duties;
- the procedures relating to the handling of contracts, loans, checks, deposits and gifts; and
- general provisions regarding the seal, fiscal year, amendments, books and records, and so on.

All appropriate forms for starting a nonprofit foundation should be reviewed, completed, and forwarded for approval to the correct governmental agencies. Check with your state nonprofit association for guidelines. Contact information for these associations is located at http://www.ncna.org.

The next crucial step is to form a board of directors that mirrors the composition of the community. Each person should be selected based on the expertise and experience he or she can bring to the foundation. You will need persons who have the knowledge and energy to achieve the goals set forth. Persons with backgrounds in fund-raising, public relations/marketing, media, community activism, and educational matters are but a few who should be given consideration. The initial board will set the tone of the organization. Ex-officio members of the board could be members of the school board or employees of the local district.

Fund Development

With a dynamic board in place, the policies and procedures should be written and committees formed. Suggestions for these include fund development, finance, publicity, community liaison, and others as needed.

Defining priorities is essential. What must be accomplished first? A strategic plan based on local educational needs should be written and approved by the board. Once in place, it should be shared with the public for support and endorsement. Community volunteers must be recruited as needed to meet the goals within the plan. A new school/community partnership can be established by involving educators, parents, businesses, professionals, and government officials to create a viable team for the advancement of local education.

A study conducted by the Public Education Network in 2000 (PEN, 2001) determined that $65 million has been raised by LEFs. Approximately $27 million was used to support teacher quality. An additional $14 million was employed for school accountability to raise standards and assessments. Interestingly, the budgets for the LEFs ranged from $23,000 to $9 million. Foundations continue to be the focal point for the generation of dollars, but corporations and individual support have also been increasing with funding from corporations constituting 15% of LEF funds. In 1996, individuals made 5% of the contributions increasing to 12% in 2000. Currently, endowments are an essential source of funding with 7 out of 10 LEFs having them, with the median being more than $90,000.

The nature of LEFs is changing. The boards are conducting assessments of their own effectiveness and also keeping administrative costs low, with approximately $9 out of every $10 directed to programs and services. They are using these funds to improve schools. In addition, the flow of information is increasing to the general public on research of student achievement and what has been effective. Twenty percent of the LEFs indicated the provision of research and other information to the media for better public understanding. Information flow is also conducted through organizing community forums and joining coalitions with other groups concerned with education. Through these and other efforts, the number of volunteers has increased, with 180,000 hours being given annually.

Diversity is reflected in several ways with LEFs through their staff and membership composition. Within the last few years the latter has moved from almost totally the business community to being more inclusive of nonprofit organizations, school district representatives, government officials, and persons with academic backgrounds.

Volunteers for Fund Development

Does the district have a sufficient number of volunteers educated in the solicitation process of meeting potential donors and asking them for large donations? If not, volunteers will need to be trained with the necessary information followed by simulated (role-playing) situations until confidence is achieved. To find volunteers for fund development, there are several methods to be employed. Individuals in various categories should be considered:

- administrators and central office staff, teachers, and parents who raise money in the community and/or religious affiliations;
- professional persons who raise funds for United Way, Boy Scouts, Girl Scouts, and other community-based organizations;

- small business owners who have grown their businesses based on customer service and satisfaction;
- persons who know marketing in the areas of insurance, financial planning, advertising, and public relations; and
- alumni of the district who know the benefits of the positive education received from the district;

When the general list has been developed, there are several necessary characteristics to keep in mind: credibility, articulation, sociability, adaptability, discretion, and resilience. For example, volunteers should be credible and willing to make a donation themselves. They must be articulate and be able to clearly state why the money is needed and how it will be used. Furthermore, the volunteers must be willing to meet new people and be adaptable to customizing their approach based on the donor's interests. They must also be discrete and respectful of the donor's privacy and resilient when experiencing rejection by a potential donor.

When the likely candidates are found, there are some suggested steps in the management of volunteers. First, prepare the Volunteer Position Description (see Appendix M). Then recruit, screen, and select the volunteers. No matter how much volunteer work each has undertaken, all must be trained on the specifics of the capital campaign under consideration. Once they begin the process of contacting and visiting with donors, volunteers need to be supervised and records kept of their service. Such ongoing evaluation is key to the progress and overall effectiveness of the campaign.

Volunteers should know that an evaluation is part of the process in fund development and is essential to the success of a volunteer management program. A form similar to the

Self-Evaluation for Volunteers (see Appendix N) should be given to each person before he or she meets with the supervisor. Keep in mind that this evaluation is to help the volunteer to reflect on his or her accomplishments and acknowledge any improvements that are needed. Volunteers should consider whether the position is meeting their needs and suggest possible ways they might want to expand their involvement. Also, ascertain how the volunteer management system is working from the volunteer's perspective. It is always good to get feedback from those directly involved in the campaign as a volunteer.

Conclusion

Knowledge of a variety of fund-raising techniques is imperative as new demands are placed on schools and districts in the 21st century. Tight budgets and additional budget cuts will make fund-raising a necessity in order to provide quality educational experiences and materials to our students, teachers, and other school personnel. Although fund-raising can be tedious and time consuming, the results reaped from successful efforts will be worth all the hard work and will possibly serve to motivate all to engage in additional fund-raising endeavors.

References

Works Cited

Allen, R. C. (1998, November 13). Why professors should learn how to be fundraisers. *The Chronicle of Higher Education, 45*(12), B4–B5.

Bauer, D. G. (2000). Making school fundraising a learning experience. *Principal, 80*(2), 13–17.

Greenfield, J. M. (1994). *Fundraising fundamentals: A guide to annual giving for professionals and volunteers.* New York: John Wiley & Sons.

Hill, J. G., & Johnson, F. (2005). *Revenues and expenditures for public elementary and secondary education: School year 2002–2003* (NCES 2005–353). Washington, DC: U.S. Department of Education, National Center for Education Statistics.

Kihlstedt, A., & Schwartz, C. P. (1997). *Capital campaigns: Strategies that work.* Gaithersburg, MD: Aspen Publishing.

Lewis, H. G. (1989). *How to write powerful fund raising letters.* Chicago, IL: Plurchies Press.

Mabry, V. (November/December, 2000). Teachers help fundraisers make the grade. *PTO Today, 2*(2). Retrieved July 15, 2005, from http://www.ptotoday.com/ 1100fundraising.html

Miner, J. T., Miner, L. E., & Griffith, J. (1998). *Proposal planning and writing* (2nd ed.). Westport, CT: Oryx Press.

National Association of Elementary School Principals (NAESP). (2000). Fund-raising a "necessary evil" for elementary schools. *NAESP News.* Retrieved July 15, 2005, from http://naesp.org/ContentLoad. do?contentId=1108

Public Education Network (PEN). (Winter 2001). Summary of PEN's 2000 annual survey. *Connections, 8* (1). Retrieved July 15, 2005, from http://www.public-education.org/pdf/Publications/Connections/2001/ Nearly_Half_of_LEF_Funding.pdf

Stephens, K. R., & Karnes, F. A. (1999). Creative ways to raise money for your gifted program. *Gifted Child Today, 22*(2), 48–51.

U.S. Department of Education (2005). *The federal role in education.* Retrieved July 10, 2005, from http://www. ed.gov/about/overview/fed/role.html

Trejos, N. (May 23, 2000). Schools turning to no-fuss fundraising online. *The Washington Post,* A1.

White, D. E. (1995). *The art of planned giving: Understanding donors and the culture of giving.* New York: John Wiley & Sons

Winter, R. (2002, February 25). Teacher can you spare a dime? *TIME Magazine, 159*(8), 20.

Resources

Web Sites

Private and Corporate Foundation Information

The Chronicle of Philanthropy—News from the nonprofit world.

http://philanthropy.com

The Council on Foundations—A nonprofit membership association of grantmaking foundations and corporations.

http://www.cof.org

Community Foundation Locator—Find grant giving agencies in your community.

http://www.communityfoundationlocator.org/search/index.cfm

The Foundation Center—Collects, organizes, analyzes, and disseminates information on foundations, corporate giving, and related subjects.

http://fdncenter.org

GuideStar—A national database of nonprofit organizations.

http://www.guidestar.org

Public Register's Annual Report Service—Company financials, including annual reports, prospectuses or 10k's on more than 3,600 public companies are available here.

http://www.prars.com

Report Gallery—Provides the annual reports of many companies

http://www.reportgallery.com

General Grant Finding Resources

Findit.org—Collection of online grantmaking resources.
http://www.findit.org/html/fund_online_foundations.html

Fundsnet—Source for grants, fund-raising, grant writing, and philanthropy information.
http://www.fundsnetservices.com

Grantmakers for Education—A membership organization for grantmakers that supports education from early childhood through K–12 and higher education.
http://edfunders.com

The Grantsmanship Center—Offers grantsmanship training and publications to nonprofit organizations and government agencies.
http://www.tgci.com

SchoolGrants—A great starting place for K–12 educators.
http://www.schoolgrants.org

Educational Organizations

Council for Advancement and Support of Education—Provides education professionals with development tools to advance their institution.
http://www.case.org

Public Education Network—Information on Local Education Funds (LEFs) and other key issues affecting student achievement in America's public schools.
http://www.publiceducation.org

Fund-Raising

American Association of Fund Raising Counsel, Inc—Offers tips on how to choose effective and ethical fund-raising counsel.
http://www.aafrc.org

The Association of Fund Raising Distributors & Suppliers (AFRDS)—An international association of companies that manufacture, supply, and distribute products that are resold by nonprofit organizations for fund-raising purposes.
http://www.afrds.org

Campbell's Labels for Education—Redeem product labels for free educational merchandise.
http://www.labelsforeducation.com

The Fundraising Bank—Has lists and links to fund-raising products, printed resources on fund-raising, a newsletter, and a fund-raising bulletin board.

http://www.fundraising-ideas.com

General Mills Boxtops for Education—Clip the Box Tops logos from more than 330 participating General Mills products, and turn them into cash for your favorite school.

http://www.boxtops4education.com

Kash for Kids—A recycling program that turns trash into cash.

http://www.kashforkids.com

National Scrip Center—A training and education support services movement that teaches organizations to raise money by purchasing goods and services using scrip.

http://www.nationalscripcenter.org/what_is_scrip.html

National Society of Fund Raising Executives—Professional association for individuals responsible for generating philanthropic support for a wide variety of not-for-profit, charitable organizations.

http://www.nsfre.org

NonprofitXpress—An online news source that focuses on news about fund-raising, management, technology, and giving and volunteering in the nonprofit sector.

http://www.npxpress.com

e-Volunteerism—a quarterly online journal that addresses volunteer issues.

http://www.e-volunteerism.com

Fund Development

Planned Giving Design Center—Includes news alert; reviews of laws pertaining to planned giving; articles discussing current issues in planned giving; and commentary and analysis on IRS pronouncements, judicial decisions, and legislative developments affecting charitable taxation.

http://www.pgdc.net

Online Compendium of Federal and State Regulations for U.S. Nonprofit Organizations—Provides a central resource for administrators, regulators, and the interested public to find information about the laws and regulations controlling nonprofit organizations in the U.S.

http://www.muridae.com/nporegulation/main.html

Funding Agencies

National Endowment for the Arts—Federal agency devoted exclusively to nurturing creativity and preserving cultural heritage through the arts.

http://arts.endow.gov

National Endowment for the Humanities—An independent grantmaking agency of the U.S. government dedicated to supporting research, education, and public programs in the humanities.

http://www.neh.fed.us

National Science Foundation (NSF)—An independent U.S. government agency responsible for promoting science and engineering through programs.
http://www.nsf.gov

U.S. Department of Education—Offers a range and an ever-growing collection of information about the Department, including initiatives and priorities, grant opportunities, publications, and research and statistics.
http://www.ed.gov

Government Publications

The Catalog of Federal Domestic Assistance (CFDA)—A government-wide compendium of federal programs, projects, services, and activities that provide assistance or benefits to the American public.
http://www.cfda.gov

Federal Register—Contains federal agency regulations; proposed rules and notices (including notices for grant applications); and executive orders, proclamations, and other Presidential documents.
http://www.gpoaccess.gov/fr

U.S. Government Printing Office (GPO)—Government documents at your fingertips.
http://www.gpoaccess.gov

Grant Writing Assistance

GrantStation—For an annual subscription, users can search

the GrantStation database of grantmakers, learn how to write effective grant proposals, and receive an e-mail newsletter.
http://www.grantstation.com

Guide for Writing a Funding Proposal—Provides both instructions on how to write a funding proposal and actual examples of a completed proposal.
http://learnerassociates.net/proposal

Books

Grant Writing

Bauer, D. G. (1998). *Educator's Internet funding guide: Classroom Connect's reference guide for technology funding*. El Segundo, CA: Classroom Connect.

Bauer, D. G. (1998). *The principal's guide to winning grants*. San Francisco: Jossey-Bass.

Bauer, D. G. (1998). *The teacher's guide to winning grants*. San Francisco: Jossey-Bass.

Bauer, D. G. (2000). *Technology funding for schools*. San Francisco: Jossey-Bass.

Browning, B. (2001). *Grant writing for dummies*. Indianapolis, IN: Wiley Publishing.

Ferguson, J. (1998). *Grants and awards for teachers: A guide to federal and private funding* (3rd ed.). Alexandria, VA: Capitol Publishing Group.

Foundation Center. (1999). *National guide to funding for elementary & secondary education*. New York: Author.

Hall, M., & Howlett, S. (2003). *Getting funded: The complete guide to writing grant proposals*. Portland, OR: Continuing Education Press.

Hall-Ellis, S. D., Meyer, D., Hoffman, F. W., & Jerabek, J. A. (1999). *Grantsmanship for small libraries and school library media centers*. Englewood, CO: Libraries Unlimited.

Karges-Bone, L. (1994). *Grant writing for teachers: If you can write a lesson plan, you can write a grant*. Carthage, IL: Good Apple.

Karsh, E., & Fox, A. S. (2003). *The only grant-writing book you'll ever need*. New York: Carroll and Graf Publishers.

Levenson, S. (2001). *How to get grants and gifts for the public schools*. Boston: Allyn and Bacon.

Ruskin, K. B., & Achilles, C. M. (1995). *Grantwriting, fundraising, and partnerships: Strategies that work*. Thousand Oaks, CA: Corwin Press.

Fund-Raising

Bancel, M. (2000). *Preparing your capital campaign*. San Francisco: Jossey-Bass.

Ciconte, B. L., & Jacob, J. (2005). *Fundraising basics: A complete guide* (2nd ed.). Sudbury, MA: Jones and Bartlett Publishers.

Gensheimer, C. F. (1993). *Raising funds for your child's school.* New York: Walker & Company.

Joachim, J. C. (2003). *Beyond the bake sale: The ultimate school fund-raising book.* New York: St. Martin's Press.

Lynn, D., & Lynn, K. (Eds.). (1996). *More great fundraising ideas for youth groups: Over 150 easy-to-use money-makers that really work.* Grand Rapids, MI: Zondervan Publishing House.

Morris, P. (2000). *A practical guide to fund-raising in schools.* New York: Routledge

Mutz, J., & Murray, K. (2000). *Fundraising for dummies.* Fostser City, CA: IDG Books Worldwide.

Foundations and Other Fund Development Strategies

Beaird, S., & Hayes, W. E. (1999). *Building an endowment: What, why, and how.* Washington, DC: National Catholic Educational Association.

Grace, K. S. (2005). *Beyond fund raising: New strategies for nonprofit innovation and investment* (2nd ed.). Hoboken, NJ: John Wiley & Sons.

Greenfield, J. M. (1999). *Fundraising: Evaluating and managing the fund development process* (2nd ed.). New York: John Wiley & Sons.

Havens, M. M. (2000) *Dream big: Creating and growing your school foundation.* Rockville, MD: National School Public Relations Association.

Joyaux, S. P. (2001). *Strategic fund development: Building profitable relationships that last* (2nd ed.). Gaithersburg, MD: Aspen Publishers.

Lant, J. (1993). *Development today: A fund raising guide for nonprofit organizations.* Cambridge, MA: Jeffrey Lant Associates.

Lowenstein, R. L., & Sorenson, A. (1997). *Pragmatic fundraising for college administrators and development officers.* Gainsville, FL: University Press of Florida.

McCormick, D. H., Bauer, D. G., & Ferguson, D. E. (2003). *Creating foundations for American schools.* Sudbury, MA: Jones and Bartlett Publishers.

Muro, J. J. (1994). *Creating and funding educational foundations: A guide for local school districts.* New York: Prentice Hall.

Nichols, J. E. (1994). *Targeted fund raising: Defining and refining your development strategy.* Chicago, IL: Precept Press.

Resources

Poderis, T. (1997). *It's a great day to fundraise! A veteran campaigner reveals the development tips and techniques that will work for you.* Willoughby Hills, OH: Fundamerica Press.

Periodicals

Advancing Philanthropy
Association of Fundraising Professionals
1101 King Street, Suite 700
Alexandria, VA 22314
Phone: (703) 684-0410
Web site: http://www.afpnet.org/publications/advancing_philanthropy

Children and Youth Funding Report
CD Publications
8204 Fenton Street
Silver Spring, MD 20910
Phone: (800) 666-6380
Web site: http://www.cdpublications.com

Contributions
Cambridge Fund Raising Associates
P.O. Box 338, Medfield, MA 02052
Newton Center, MA 02159
Phone: (508) 359-0019
Web site: http://www.contributionsmagazine.com

Council for Advancement and Support of Education
1307 New York Ave., NW, Ste. 1000
Washington, DC 20005

Phone: (202) 328-2273
Web site: http://www.case.org

Foundation News & Commentary
Council on Foundations
1828 L Street, NW
Washington, DC 20036
Phone: (202) 466-6512
Web site: http://www.foundationnews.org

Grassroots Fundraising Journal
Chardon Press
3781 Broadway
Oakland, CA 94611
Phone: (888) 458-8588
Web site: http://www.grassrootsfundraising.org

State Funding Report
Thompson Publishing Group, Inc.
Government Information Services
Education Funding Research Council
1725 K Street, NW, Suite 700
Washington, DC 20006
Phone: (800) 444-8741
Web site: http://www.thompson.com/libraries/grantseeking/stat/index.html

Technology Funding Bulletin
7920 Norfolk Ave., Ste. 900
Bethesda, MD 20814
Phone: (800) 394-0115
Web site: www.eschoolnews.org

Needs Survey

Please indicate what you consider to be the top three areas of need in our school (1, 2, 3). If you perceive a need not listed, please record it under additional need.

_____ Assessment/testing (specify) _____

_____ Athletic equipment (specify) _____

_____ Audiovisual equipment (specify) _____

_____ Classroom/instructional materials (specify) _____

_____

_____ Computers (specify) _____

_____ Field experiences (specify) _____

_____ Library books (specify) _____

_____ Playground equipment (specify)_____

_____ Professional development (specify) _____

_____ Science equipment (specify) _____

_____ Software (specify) _____

Additional needs _____

_____

_____

_____

_____

I am a:

- ❏ Student
- ❏ Former student
- ❏ Parent
- ❏ Teacher/grade ____ subject area_____
- ❏ Other school personnel
- ❏ Other (please specify)

Thank you for your input.

Needs Survey

Please indicate the three most important areas you consider as significant needs for our school. For example, if you feel that students would benefit from a larger variety of instructional materials in science class, you would indicate that as an important need. Please be specific.

_____

_____

_____

_____

_____

_____

_____

_____

_____

_____

_____

_____

I am a:

- ❏ Student
- ❏ Former student
- ❏ Parent
- ❏ Teacher/grade _____   subject area_____
- ❏ Other school personnel
- ❏ Other (please specify)

Thank you for your input.

Appendix C: Funding Agency Prospect

GENERAL INFORMATION
Name
Address
Phone
Web address
Contact person
FINANCIAL INFORMATION
Number of grants funded per year
Average grant size
Period of funding
FOCUS AREAS
Subject(s)/Topic(s)
Population
Geographic
Recipient(s)
APPLICATION INFORMATION
Letter of inquiry required?
Necessary application forms?
Deadlines?
Meeting dates?
NOTES

Appendix D: Application for Federal Education Assistance

Application for **F**ederal **E**ducation **A**ssistance (ED 424)	U.S. Department of Education Form Approved OMB No. 1890-0017 Exp. OMB Approved

Applicant Information

1. Name and Address

Legal Name: _____

Address: _____

Organizational Unit

City | State | County | ZIP Code + 4

2. Applicant's D-U-N-S Number

3. Applicant's T-I-N

4. Catalog of Federal Domestic Assistance #: 8 4

Title: _____

5. Project Director: _____

Address: _____

City | State | ZIP Code + 4

Tel. #: _____   Fax #: _____

E-Mail Address: _____

6. Novice Applicant ☐ Yes ☐ No

7. Is the applicant delinquent on any Federal debt? ☐ Yes ☐ No

(If "Yes," attach an explanation.)

8. Type of Applicant *(Enter appropriate letter in the box.)*

A State
B Local
C Special District
D Indian Tribe
E Individual
F Independent School District

G Public College or University
H Private, Non-Profit College or University
I Non-Profit Organization
J Private, Profit-Making Organization
K Other *(Specify):*

9. State Application Identifier: _____

Application Information

10. Type of Submission:

—*PreApplication*
☐ Construction
☐ Non-Construction

—*Application*
☐ Construction
☐ Non-Construction

11. Is application subject to review by Executive Order 12372 process?

☐ Yes *(Date made available to the Executive Order 12372 process for review):* _____

☐ No *(If "No," check appropriate box below.)*

☐ Program is not covered by E.O. 12372.

☐ Program has not been selected by State for review.

12. Proposed Project Dates: **Start Date:**   **End Date:**

13. Are any research activities involving human subjects planned at any time during the proposed project period?

☐ Yes (Go to 13a.)   ☐ No (Go to item 14.)

13a. Are **all** the research activities proposed designated to be exempt from the regulations?

☐ Yes (Provide Exemption(s) #):

☐ No (Provide Assurance #):

14. Descriptive Title of Applicant's Project:

Estimated Funding

15a. Federal	$	.00
b. Applicant	$	.00
c. State	$	.00
d. Local	$	.00
e. Other	$	.00
f. Program Income	$	.00
g. TOTAL	$	0 .00

Authorized Representative Information

16. To the best of my knowledge and belief, all data in this preapplication/application are true and correct. The document has been duly authorized by the governing body of the applicant and the applicant will comply with the attached assurances if the assistance is awarded.

a. Authorized Representative *(Please type or print name clearly.)*

b. Title

c. Tel. #: _____   Fax #: _____

d. E-Mail Address:

e. Signature of Authorized Representative   Date:

GOALS AND OBJECTIVES	PERSONS RESPONSIBLE AND QUALIFICATIONS	TIMELINE IN MONTHS

Appendix F: Plan of Operation/
Plan of Evaluation Blank Template

Objective:			
Activities and Personnel Responsible	Timeline (Months)	Evaluation Criteria	Evaluation Indicators

PERSONNEL	YEAR 1	YEAR 2	YEAR 3

U.S. DEPARTMENT OF EDUCATION
BUDGET INFORMATION
NON-CONSTRUCTION PROGRAMS

OMB Control Number: 1890-0004
Expiration Date: 10-31-2007

Name of Institution/Organization

Applicants requesting funding for only one year should complete the column under "Project Year 1." Applicants requesting funding for multi-year grants should complete all applicable columns. Please read all instructions before completing form.

SECTION A - BUDGET SUMMARY
U.S. DEPARTMENT OF EDUCATION FUNDS

Budget Categories	Project Year 1 (a)	Project Year 2 (b)	Project Year 3 (c)	Project Year 4 (d)	Project Year 5 (e)	Total (f)
1. Personnel						
2. Fringe Benefits						
3. Travel						
4. Equipment						
5. Supplies						
6. Contractual						
7. Construction						
8. Other						
9. Total Direct Costs (lines 1-8)						
10. Indirect Costs*						
11. Training Stipends						
12. Total Costs (lines 9-11)						

***Indirect Cost Information (To Be Completed by Your Business Office):**

If you are requesting reimbursement for indirect costs on line 10, please answer the following questions:

(1) Do you have an Indirect Cost Rate Agreement approved by the Federal government? ____ Yes ____ No

(2) If yes, please provide the following information:

Period Covered by the Indirect Cost Rate Agreement: From: ___/___/___ To: ___/___/___ (mm/dd/yyyy)

Approving Federal agency: ____ ED ____ Other (please specify): _____

(3) For Restricted Rate Programs (check one) -- Are you using a restricted indirect cost rate that:

____ Is included in your approved Indirect Cost Rate Agreement? or ____ Complies with 34 CFR 76.564(c)(2)?

Name of Institution/Organization

Applicants requesting funding for only one year should complete the column under "Project Year 1." Applicants requesting funding for multi-year grants should complete all applicable columns. Please read all instructions before completing form.

SECTION B - BUDGET SUMMARY
NON-FEDERAL FUNDS

Budget Categories	Project Year 1 (a)	Project Year 2 (b)	Project Year 3 (c)	Project Year 4 (d)	Project Year 5 (e)	Total (f)
1. Personnel						
2. Fringe Benefits						
3. Travel						
4. Equipment						
5. Supplies						
6. Contractual						
7. Construction						
8. Other						
9. Total Direct Costs (Lines 1-8)						
10. Indirect Costs						
11. Training Stipends						
12. Total Costs (Lines 9-11)						

SECTION C – BUDGET NARRATIVE (see instructions)

ED 524

Appendix I: Budget Planning Worksheet Blank Template

BUDGET CATEGORY	YEAR 1	YEAR 2	YEAR 3
Personnel			
Equipment			
Supplies			
Communications			
Travel			

Appendix J: Creative Fund-Raising Ideas

Academic Marathons
Activity Fee
Adopt-a-_____
Advertisements
Alumni
    Contributions
Annual Event
Art Show
A-Thon
Auction
Bake Sale
Balloon Release
Banquet
Bazaar
Bee
Bike-A-Thon
Bingo
Birthday Newsletter
Blind Auction
Book Fair
Booster Campaign
Bowling Night
Breakfast
Brick Engraving
Brunch
Bumper Sticker Sale
Business
    Contributions
Calendars
Candle Sale
Candy Sale
Capital Campaign
Car Wash
Caroling
Carnival
Celebrity Event
Comedy Night
Competition
Concert/Performance
Concession Stand
Consignment Sale
Contest
Cookbook
Cookie Dough Sale
Cook-Off
Corporate Collection
Coupon Book
Craft Fair
Creating and Selling
    Books
Curb Painting
Dance
Debate
Decorations

Dessert Night
Dessert Theater
Dinner
Direct Mail
Direct Sales
Direct Solicitation
Discount Card
Donation Can
Donations
Dramatic Production
Drawing
Dress-Down or
    Dress-Up Day
Duck Race
Face Painting
Faculty/Alumni
    Game
Faculty/Student
    Game
Fair
Fall Festival
Family Night
Family Portrait Sale
Fashion Show
Festival
Field Day
Flower Sale
Fund Raiser
    Insurance
Gala
Game Night
Get Out of Class
    Card
Gift Certificate
Gift Market
Gift Wrap Sale
Gift Wrapping
Gourmet Item Sale
Grab Bag Sale
Grandparent's Day
Grant Writing
Greeting Cards
Grocery Coupons
Guessing Game (Jar
    of Coins, Teacher's
    Age)
Hat Day
Haunted House
Historical Afghans
History Bee
Holiday Store
Home Tours
Hug-O-Gram or
    Smile-O-Gram

Ice Cream Social
International Dinner
Internet Purchasing
Jail
Jog-A-Thon
Jump-A-Thon
Karaoke Contest
Kidnap the Principal
Kiss a Pig
Label and Receipt
    Programs
Lawn Decorations
Letter From Santa
Luncheon
Magazine
    Subscriptions
Magic Show
Marathon
Mascot Tattoos
Mathematics Bee
Money Tree
Movies
Music Sale
Musical
Mystery Dinner
Online Fundraising
Pageant
Parade
Parent Production
Parent's Night Out
Party
Penny Drive
Pizza Kits
Play
Pledges
Phone Campaign
Plant Sale
Poinsettia Sale
Popcorn Sale
Portion of Profit
    Programs
Poster Sale
Potluck
Pre-Sale Catalog
Product Sale
PTA Membership
    Drive
Quarter Rally
Raffle
Read-A-Thon
Reception
Recycling
Rock-A-Thon
Rummage Sale

Run
Safety Product Sale
School Newspaper
School Planners
School Spirit Items
School Store
School-Business
    Partnerships
Science Bee
Scratch Cards
Scrip
Selling Ads
Sidewalk Sale
Silent Auction
Singing Telegrams
Snack Sale
Software Sale
Special Event
Spelling Bee
Spiral Wishing Well
Spiritwear
Sponsor Sheet
Sports Activity/
    Tournament
Stage Production
Student Pictures
Tailgate Party
Talent Show
Teacher Follies
Telethon
Theme Baskets
Themed Dinner
Tournament
Trees
Trivia Night
T-shirt Sale
Used Sporting Good
    Sale
Valentines
Vending Machines
Video Sale
Wall of Recognition
Wall Painting
White Elephant Store
Winterfest
Wish List
Work for Donations
Yard Sale
Yearbook
Yearbook Ads

Appendix K: Creative Fund-Raising Timeline

Month	Objective	Activities	Person Responsible	Due Date	Expected Outcome
August					
September					
October					
November					
December					
January					
February					
March					
April					
May					
June					
July					

Appendix L: Sample Donor Identification Form

General Information

Name: _____

Address: _____

City: _____

State: _____ Zip: _____

Home Phone:_____ Work Phone: _____

Fax: _____ E-mail: _____

Birthdate:_____ Birth Place: _____

Marital Status and Family

❑ Married ❑ Divorced ❑ Widow/Widower ❑ Single

Has spouse attended local schools? ❑ Yes ❑ No

If yes, which ones: _____

_____

# of Children: _____

Names: _____

_____

Are they currently enrolled in our elementary/secondary schools? ❑

Yes ❑ No

If yes, which one(s) _____

Child	School
_____	_____
_____	_____
_____	_____

Employment History

Current Employment

Position: _____

Company: _____

Address: _____

Work Phone: _____Fax: _____

Previous Employment_____

Position: _____

Company: _____

Address: _____

Appendix L, continued

Relationship to Local School/District

Giving History to School/District: _____
Amount: _____
Purpose: _____
Volunteer Positions: _____

Affiliations

Professional Membership(s): _____
Club Membership(s): _____
Social Affiliation(s): _____
Religious Affiliation: _____
Special Interests: _____

Known Giving to Other Organizations

Organization _____
Amount: _____ Date _____
Known Wealth _____
Property: _____
Stocks: _____
Estimated Annual Salary: _____
Estimated Annual Income: _____

Potential Level of Funding and Interest

Potential Level: _____
Interest(s): _____

Who Should Approach the Donor?

Name: _____
Relationship: _____

Appendix M: Volunteer Position Description

Position title: _____

Description of responsibilities: _____

_____

Time commitment: _____

Skills/knowledge/experience needed for the position: ___

_____

_____

Requirements: _____

_____

Training needed: _____

_____

Importance of the position: _____

_____

Position: _____

Supervisor: _____

Position description prepared by: _____

Date: _____

Appendix N: Self-Evaluation Form for Volunteers

The _____ School District appreciates your time and services during the capital campaign. To get ready for our evaluation meeting, please complete the following form.

Why did I choose to be a volunteer for the capital campaign?_____
_____
_____

I can improve my performance in the following three ways: _____
_____
_____

How have I been able to fulfill my commitment as a volunteer for the capital campaign? _____
_____

What items in the position description took the most time? _____
_____
_____

Were there additional responsibilities that are not in the position description?
_____
_____

What could we do to help you improve your responsibilities in the capital campaign? What support will you need? _____
_____
_____

Please describe the supervision you received on the assignment. _____
_____
_____

How helpful was the training you received and were there areas which should have been included, but were not?_____
_____
_____

Do you wish to continue to volunteer for fund development for the school district?   Yes   No

Why or why not? _____
_____

Additional Comments:_____
_____
_____

Printed in the United States
by Baker & Taylor Publisher Services